THE STORY OF DARKNESS

Studies in Austrian Literature, Culture, and Thought

Translation Series

Gerhard Roth

The Story of Darkness

Translated by
Helga Schreckenberger
and Jacqueline Vansant
Afterword by
Helga Schreckenberger

ARIADNE PRESS
Riverside, California

Ariadne Press would like to express its appreciation to the Austrian Cultural Institute, New York and the Bundeskanzleramt – Sektion Kunst, Vienna for their assistance in publishing this book.

Translated from the German *Die Geschichte der Dunkelheit* by arrangement with S. Fischer Verlag GmbH, Frankfurt am Main
© 1991 S. Fischer Verlag GmbH, Frankfurt am Main

Library of Congress Cataloging-in-Publication Data

Roth, Gerhard, 1942 June 24-
    [Geschichte der Dunkelheit. English]
    The story of darkness / Gerhard Roth : translated by Helga Schreckenberger and Jacqueline Vansant ; afterword by Helga Schreckenberger.
            p.   cm. -- (Studies in Austrian literature, culture, and thought. Translation series)
    ISBN 1-57241-070-1
    1. Vienna (Austria)--Biography. 2. Antisemitism--Austria--Vienna--History--20th century. 3. Jews--Austria--Vienna--Biography. 4. Refugees, Jewish--Great Britain--Biography. I. Schreckenberger, Helga. II. Vansant, Jacqueline, 1954- . III. Title. IV. Series.
DS135.A93R6913   1999
943.6'1300492'092--dc21
[B]   98-46971
                                                       CIP

Cover Design:
Art Director, Designer: George McGinnis

I

After having lived in the country for ten years, I moved to Vienna and into the apartment of a former fellow student of mine named Ascher. During the same time period, he committed suicide in my house on the Yugoslavian border.

I quit medical school after my third year to become a writer. Ascher became a doctor, practicing first in Vienna, then at the Regional Hospital in Graz. From time to time I would receive a letter from him in which he reacted to one of my books. Whenever we met, he talked about Austria, a country that made him suffer, but which he also loved to an extent I've never seen before or since. He always wanted to hear particulars – particulars about political developments, about life among the farmers, but especially about Austrian history – about the "suppressed nightmare," as he called it. He never visited me in my house. He didn't want to "disturb" me. The truth of the matter is he was a true urbanite who felt lost in the country and in nature.

"If I were forced to be a country doctor, I would shoot myself," he exclaimed now and then. He did shoot himself with a hunting rifle, and I can't forgive myself for not having taken him seriously. Ascher was a scrupulous person, an indecisive brooder. It's all the more absurd that he, of all people, was found guilty of malpractice. Even before the case was beaten to death in the local Graz paper, the *Kleine Zeitung*, he called me and told me about the unfortunate accident that had caused the death of an eleven-year-old boy. He said he had murdered a human being. No matter how you looked at it, it had been murder. A few weeks later he wrote and suggested that since he had lost his position at the Regional Hospital I should move into his empty apartment in Vienna and sublet the house I rented to him. Since I had intended to go to Vienna anyway, the "hydrocephalus of Austria," as the capital is called in the provinces, I agreed immediately.

In Vienna I started writing articles about Austrian politics and history for German newspapers. That later earned me the title of traitor, as if you could free-lance for Austrian newspapers without dropping below the poverty line. From the very beginning I intended to write a novel about Austria, about the open insanity of the Austrian past and the hidden madness of Austria's everyday life. However, it was Ascher's suicide that motivated me to take up my work.

Ascher's apartment was on Döblingerstraße. My first walk led me to Währing Park which borders on an abandoned Jewish cemetery. It was November and the leaves were falling from the trees that rose up along the fallen tombstones. A flock of crows was sitting on the branches. The cemetery was surrounded by a wall extending from a house with bricked-up windows. This cemetery gave me the idea for my first project, namely, writing the life story of an Austrian Jew who had left Vienna in 1938 and returned after World War II. In Austria the prevailing belief is that exiles were comparatively lucky people who enjoyed themselves abroad. Naturally none of them were welcome after the war. The Austrian Jews were not only robbed blind by the rest of the population in 1938 but also taken advantage of and cheated because of their desperate situation (before their flight abroad — that is, if they were able to escape). In the best case scenario the price for their property was haggled down low. Like their Austrian business partners the refugees knew that chicken feed was better than nothing. The governor of Carinthia could tell you a thing or two about that, since the property that he inherited came from such dubious and dirty machinations. Many apartments in the second district now inhabited by Viennese did so as well.

In my free time I visited all the places where Jews had lived before the Nazis marched into Austria, especially the second district, Leopoldstadt. I liked to walk through Leopoldstadt, although now it's a depressing district, a sad one, seemingly deserted. I studied Jewish Vienna for more than four years — the temples that were burned down in the so-called *Kristallnacht*, the coffeehouses and stores that have since "disappeared," and finally the mentality that led to the destruction of Jewish life in Austria. When I met Karl Berger in 1987, he was sixty-eight years old.

I made his acquaintance through my publisher, after having been unsuccessful in my search for an exile who had returned. After our first conversation we started meeting regularly, mostly in his apartment. It was in his little kitchen that I recorded in several notebooks what he told me about his life. I am reproducing these notes, which I edited without making any major changes, because I believe that Berger's reports are so exemplary that they transcend the boundaries of documents and literature.

II

My Ancestors

My maternal great-grandfather's name was Jakob Edelmann. In his old age he liked to sit on a bench on an avenue in front of Augarten Park in Vienna. He looked well dressed in his silk caftan and elegant black hat. In particular I remember his white beard. Most of the time he spoke with acquaintances who happened to pass by. Originally he had owned a farm and a hostel near Sarajevo frequented by soldiers from the nearby garrison. One of his daughters fell in love with an officer who wasn't Jewish, and when Jakob refused to give his consent to their marriage, the officer shot his love and then himself. As a result, Jakob's first wife was so despondent that she drowned herself in the Drina. Jakob himself then became Orthodox. All his life he wore a yarmulke, the round flat skullcap (even under his hat). Later, in Vienna, where he had moved after his daughter's death and his wife's suicide, he founded a synagogue on Karmelitermarkt which was called *Machiskei Hadas*, literally "keeping the faith." After he had opened a small antique store, he married a second time, this time the widow Käthe Bienenfeld, who brought two sons into the marriage, Jacques and Joseph. After they had immigrated to France, the two sons gained dubious notoriety in Austria's monarchist circles. They bought up the jewels of the impoverished imperial couple Karl and Zita who had abdicated. Jacques and Joseph were only willing to pay for the true value of the gold and gems (Jacques and Joseph were not practicing Jews). Later they were charged with taking advantage of the unfortunate predicament of the imperial couple but were acquitted and became very wealthy. However, they were ostracized by the family until Hitler came to power. Only then did members of the family reconcile.

My grandfather, Simon Venetianer, who married Dorothea Edelmann, Jakob's only daughter by his second marriage, especially didn't want to have anything to do with Jacques and Joseph Bienenfeld. He was an Austrian monarchist. His parents owned some land and a sawmill in Slovakia. My grandfather would most likely have stayed there if he hadn't been attacked by a drunken Slovakian administrator who disparagingly called him a Jew. Simon defended himself and killed the man. After that he escaped to Vienna, whence he continued on to Budapest. (He alternated residence between these two cities for the rest of his life.) When the dust finally settled after the affair, he opened a crate factory on Franz Josef Quay in Vienna. Later he sold it in order to dedicate himself to his writing. My grandfather was an educated man. He spoke Latin and Greek and wrote under the pen name Vineta for the *Pester Lloyd*, a German-language newspaper in Budapest. In addition he lectured in *Scholle*, where Karl Kraus also spoke. He was the black sheep of the family. He had left the Jewish faith and become a free thinker. He didn't earn much from being a writer. He lived off the money he had received from the sale of his factory as well as from his inheritance. As a member of the Polar Bear Club he swam across the Danube several times during the winter – he strove to emulate the old Roman maxim *mens sana in corpore sano*, "a sound mind in a sound body." Gina Venetianer, my mother, was the only child from his marriage with Dorothea Edelmann. Simon wasn't a good father. He treated his daughter badly. For punishment he often made her kneel on dried peas. He even did this once during a visit from the Austrian writer Franz Karl Ginzkey, with whom he liked to play chess and talk all night long. Simon had wanted a son and couldn't get over the fact that he had a daughter. Conversely, he revered his wife all his life, even though he divorced her after he had bought war bonds in support of the Habsburg monarchy. To buy the bonds he had even put up his house as collateral. Having lost everything, he couldn't support his family any longer. Nonetheless he remained on friendly terms with Dorothea until his death. During World War I Simon met my future father, Adolf Berger, a lieutenant in the royal and imperial army, and invited him into his home. Adolf Berger came from a region in the Tatra Mountains, Miklos, in Slovakia. He was the youngest of a not very well-to-do family of nine boys and one girl. Over the years the members of the family ventured all over the world – to Budapest, Vienna, and even America. My father was a sales representative for Bernhard Altmann Knitwear and was in charge of the Vienna area. He was competent and proper, and envied because of his position. Even during the time between World War I and World War II when the unemployment rate was at its peak, he managed to keep his job. His good reputation is proved by the fact that after World War II Bernhard Altmann sent me ten pounds from Switzerland. I had asked him for the money I needed to obtain British citizenship.

Adolf Berger married my mother Gina when she was eighteen. In addition to me they had a daughter Edith, called Ditta. Today she is widowed and lives in Marienbad.

Childhood

I was born in Vienna on January 27, 1919. My earliest memories are fragmented and general in nature.

In the summer I would go with my parents to my father's relatives in Slovakia. That's where the so-called "country Jews" lived and ran small farms. At that time there was a Jewish community in every Slovakian town. Their livelihood consisted mainly of keeping chickens and geese; I still remember how the animals were fattened up. I also remember all the languages: you could hear German, Slovak, and Hungarian. The Jews were, for the most part, more pious than the Viennese Jews. They went to temple regularly and obeyed the religious laws more strictly. After World War I, when the monarchy collapsed, my father became a Czech citizen, which he remained until his death. We children were also Czech citizens, like many Jews in Vienna.

Our apartment was small. It consisted of a small bedroom, a hallway, a kitchen, a toilet, and a larger room. Since we had no bathing facilities, once a week we went to *Tröpferlbad*, a privately owned public bathhouse. Sometimes my uncle took me to a steam bath.

My father was very strict. Times were hard, and he was not mentally strong enough to withstand the pressures of daily life.

My parents' apartment was on the second floor, which means that it was above both the first floor and the mezzanine, a Viennese peculiarity which supposedly was done to circumvent an old construction regulation. (It's said that since the authorities in the eight-eenth century only allowed five-story buildings within the city limits, the building contractors who lived from these rentals in-vented the "half-floor" beneath the second floor. As a result, the buildings were five stories high according to the blueprints, but in reality they were six stories.) Our street, on which mainly Jews lived, belonged to Baron Schoeller, a wealthy banker. Today the area would be called "lower middle class." We used to play in the street because there was hardly any traffic. We played soccer, two on two.

Sometime before 1934 my father took me to the Sunday soccer games of the Jewish club *Hakoah* (Strength). I remember some of the players: Katz, Löwi, Scheuer, Mausner, and Dornenfeld. The agile Oppenheimer was goalie. Of course the spectators yelled anti-Semitic epithets, especially when *Hakoah* played the Vienna Sport Club. Anyhow, Orthodox Jews never went to soccer games.

When I was even younger, we liked to play a type of hop-scotch. It consisted of eight squares which were either drawn on the tarred or paved sidewalk with chalk or already etched into the pavement. The two squares on top were called "heaven" and "hell." The first player threw a small stone on square one and jumped over it on one leg. Starting from the second square, he hopped on all the others. Of course, you had to jump over "hell," whereas you could put both legs on "heaven." After jumping on all the squares, you threw the stone onto square two and jumped from the start to square three, the next time you threw the stone to square three and tried to jump to four, and so on. If you made a mistake, it was the next child's turn. The game board looked like this:

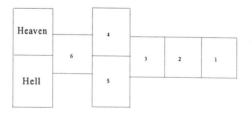

We also played all the old circle games: "Let the robbers march through the golden bridge. Where do you come from? From the Black Sea. Why are you so black?" and "Is the black cook in?" and "Rabbit in the hole." To play the game "Is the black cook in?" you walked in a circle and sang. One child ran outside the circle in the opposite direction. When the words "come along" were sung, the child on the outside touched one of the children who was walking in the circle. This child then had to follow the other child outside. The game lasted until only one child was left. The others danced around him or her and sang:

> Is the black cook in?
> No, no, no!
> Three times I have to march around,
> The fourth time I'll lose my head,
> The fifth time means: come along!
> Is the black cook in?
> Yes, yes, yes!
> There she is, there she is!
> Yuck, yuck, yuck!

I still know most of the verses by heart: "Little rabbit sat in the hole and slept. Poor little rabbit, you are so sick that you can't hop anymore. Little rabbit hop, little rabbit hop, little rabbit hop."

One child was the little rabbit, the others walked around it and sang. When the child squatting heard the words "little rabbit hop," he or she hopped towards another child who then had to take over as the sick rabbit. When we played "cops and robbers," a Jewish group was the robbers and the others the cops, or the other way around. The robbers were sent away and given a head start so they could hide. Then, and only then, were the cops allowed to look for the robbers. To catch the robbers the cops had to slap them on the back three times. It often got rough when we were the robbers and had to be arrested.

We also rode scooters made of wood, played with a yo-yo, or, like my sister, *diabolo*. *Diabolo* consisted of a bobbin and two sticks which were fastened to strings. You threw the bobbin in the air and caught it again with the strings. My sister was very good at it. She also liked to play with her doll, and I had a clown (*Kasperl*) whom I took to bed with me.

I liked to play soccer best of all. The ball would often fall into the nearby Danube Canal, and then we had to get it out of the water. The Park-on-the-Quay was situated on the city side of the canal between the Holland Bridge and the Augarten Bridge, on today's Franz Josef Quay. For us at that time it was "the world." The fish market was located down on the quay. When the ball flew down the bank towards the water, the policemen came after us. We called them the *Schmier*, a word that comes from the Hebrew word *schmira* meaning "guard." Even the Christians in Vienna still call the police *Schmier*. Playing soccer in the park was forbidden, but we did it anyway, playing from dawn until dusk. In the summer, we also went swimming in the canal between the Sweden Bridge and the Urania Bridge that was known as the "stream bath." The water was clean, but ice cold. The fish wholesalers stood on the bank. Their fish were in crates anchored in the water. The sight of the creatures scared me. Nonetheless, I felt compelled to look at the fish in the crates again and again. They were mainly carp, but there were some eels, too . . . One time when I was already in elementary school, the entire Danube Canal was frozen over. The ice-floes had stacked up one on top of the other. We children were forbidden to climb on them.

In the winter the chestnut roasters hawked their goods. They stood outside with their little iron stoves. They wore huge mittens while they roasted potatoes and chestnuts that they wrapped in cones made from newspaper. In the summer they were replaced by ice cream salesmen. In addition Bosnians with their large red fezzes sold Turkish honey with nuts and coconut lollipops at the entrance to the park. Towards the late afternoon the newspaper salesmen appeared with the *Abend*. Chairs were set up in the park, on which the mothers — mainly Jewish women — sat. They gossiped among themselves, and the woman in charge of the chairs collected the rental fees for the chairs. I didn't like to go to

Augarten Park. It seemed too dark to me. I called it suicide park.

Most families shopped at the market on Karmelitermarkt. I still remember the merchant families: the Chachamowics, the Deaks. Mrs. Deak had a booth with cheese, butter, and eggs. She was gassed by the Nazis. The Chachamowics had chickens they slaughtered right on the spot, something I never wanted to see. I only watched the fish that were for sale. They were chopped up alive after they had been scaled – it was disgusting. There were also eels . . . The vegetable dealer's name was Mathias, a jolly, elderly man: he sold spinach, potatoes, radishes, and lettuce . . . But Jews weren't the only ones who sold their wares at the market.

At that time the main conveyances were horse-drawn carts. During *Mardi gras* they were decorated with paper ribbons. In addition there were bikes and later, when I was in elementary school, trucks. The buildings in Leopoldstadt were lower than those in other districts. Many streets were dark, but there were craftsmen everywhere selling their goods in front of their stores. Some of them had their workshops in the courtyards behind the buildings; these courtyards were typical of Leopoldstadt. In the summer the shoemakers, carpenters, and paper-hangers worked outside. People had more time back then, and in any one street everyone knew everybody's name. Diagonally across from my grandmother's house was the Church of the Carmelites. During the *Corpus Christi* processions I always looked out of the window. Although I was impressed by these processions, I was aware of the tension they created. Advised not to go into the street, I watched everything from the window. I saw the splendid baldachin and the monstrance that was carried by the priest dressed in a clerical robe. Nuns followed them and children scattered flowers. I was frightened when I saw this. Leopoldstadt was a Jewish quarter, and we felt that these people were OUTSIDERS, not exactly hostile, but also not one with us.

My grandmother Dorothea was a beautiful woman with white hair and a Slavic face. Most of the time when she talked to me she told me about her life in Bosnia. On all high holidays she went to the synagogue, and on Friday evening she blessed the candles.

Actually my grandmother raised me. She was closer to me than my parents. At home I heard my mother moaning during the night as if she were being tortured, but it was only a passionate embrace. At my grandmother's there was peace and security.

Behind the house where she lived there was a small yard for the residents where I played with snails and made them race against each other. Everything was very peaceful. My grandmother was, as I said, divorced. She lived with her sister and my uncle Elias Diener, who had a stationer's store on Lilienbrunngasse. My grandmother managed their household for them. In the winter I went skating at the rink behind Sperlgasse, with "screw-steamers," as we called the blades you screwed on your shoes. My father, by the way, was a traditional, but not an Orthodox, Jew; by that I mean he considered himself Jewish but didn't follow the tenets of the faith strictly. I wasn't brought up to be religious either. For a long time I didn't consider myself a Jew, but an Austrian, even if I was a Czech citizen.

There were four *shuls,* or prayer rooms, in the courtyards on Lilienbrunngasse where my uncle had his stationer's store. Each consisted of just one room, but the rooms were crowded or packed full. All day long you could hear the unrhythmic singsong of the prayers, which didn't sound as melodious as in the synagogue but like a jumble of voices. There were prayer rooms all over Leopoldstadt. And on the high holy days rooms for celebrations were rented, for example, the Tabor movie theater next to the Hotel Stefani. In front of the Schiff Shul, the meeting hall on Schiffgasse, I once saw the funeral of a Hasidic rabbi. (Hasidim means "the pious." Hasidism is a popular, mystical-religious movement within Judaism which originated in the Ukraine, and a rabbi — literally "my teacher" — is a scholar. He is one who has studied above all else the TORAH, that is, the five books of Moses, and the Talmud, that is, the commentary to the Bible.) More than a thousand Orthodox or strictly religious Jews were standing in the street . . . The rabbi's students had come from foreign countries to attend the funeral, some even came from very far away . . . Crying, they touched the coffin and formed a huge unwieldy funeral procession . . . I'll never forget the crying and screaming. Almost all participants at the funeral spoke Yiddish. I had an aversion to Yiddish then and still do today   . . . We weren't allowed to speak Yiddish at home . . . It was, my father said, slang and not a proper language.

About Judaism

C hristians usually have either misconceptions of Judaism or no conceptions of it at all. In Judaism there is a struggle between religious and rational forces. For a while one dominates, then they meld together again. The fundamental law is to recognize the ONE AND ONLY and his demands for ethical behavior. The rules every Jew has to follow are contained in the Holy Scriptures of the Torah (teaching), the five books of Moses. The requirements for the implementation of these principles are prescribed in two collections, the Mishna (repetition), which was completed 200 years A.D., and the Gemara (completion), completed about 500 A.D. Together, the Mishna and the Gemara form the Talmud, which means "study" or "instruction." Jewish family life is determined to a great extent by religion. The highest holy day and climax of each week – like Sunday for Christians – is the Sabbath. It starts on Friday at sunset and ends Saturday when the stars come out. It's a day of rest to commemorate the creation of the world. Passover, the commemoration of the liberation of the Israelites from Egyptian bondage, is celebrated in March or April, depending on the calendar. Forty-nine days later, Shavuof marks Moses's receiving the tablets with the commandments. Rosh Hashanah, the Jewish New Year, Yom Kippur, the Day of Atonement, and Sukkoth, the Feast of Tabernacles, which commemorates the journey of the children of Israel through the desert, follow in September and October. In December, Hanukkah or the Festival of Lights commemorates the rededication of the Holy Temple, and in February or March Purim or the Feast of Lots is held to mark the deliverance of the Jews from Persian persecution. Jewish life follows strict rules.

Circumcisions take place on the eighth day after birth and are held in connection with the naming of the newborn boys. It's the sign of the covenant between a Jew and God. Bar Mitzvah, the "confirmation" of boys, is celebrated at the end of their thirteenth year (with it the boys become adults or "bound to the law"). From that point on, during morning prayer, they will wear the tallith, the prayer coat (in which they will also be buried), a square shawl made from wool or silk with tassels on each corner, and the tefillin, the prayer straps. They are worn on the left arm, opposite the heart, and on the forehead. Hands and arms are considered the tools of action; the forehead signifies the world of thought. Little cubes are fastened to the black leather straps with four sheets of parchment inscribed with four sections from the Torah. (In the Jewish faith, one's exterior is supposed to influence one's interior.) The wives of Orthodox Eastern European Jews cover their hair, some with a wig (*sheitel*) and a scarf. Occasionally there are those who have shaved their heads. During the Middle Ages wise men determined that a woman's hair holds a forbidden attraction for male strangers. None of my relatives wore a *sheitel*, and we often didn't observe the morning prayer either.

The Sabbath was always wonderful because it was so peaceful. According to our faith, on that day every Jew "receives" an extra soul which leaves him again in the evening of the next day. It's strictly forbidden to work on the Sabbath. The rules are highly complicated; even smoking isn't allowed because lighting a cigarette means making fire and is therefore considered work. It's also forbidden to walk more than 2000 meters out of the city, thus no hiking. The Talmud contains a list of "forty minus one main tasks" that are forbidden on the Sabbath. For example, it's forbidden to write two letters of the alphabet or to erase something in order to write any two letters of the alphabet. All rules are derived from the five books of Moses — which include dietary rules.

All food that conforms to Jewish dietary laws is called kosher. The laws start with the separation of meat dishes and milk dishes, which may not be eaten together at the same meal, as is put forth in the books Exodus and Deuteronomy: "You should not cook the little goat in its mother's milk." The Jewish kitchen contains *fleyshik* (meat) and *milkhik* (dairy) pots, plates, and silverware, and *parve* or neutral utensils for foods with neutral character like fish and eggs. It's generally forbidden to eat blood. In the Bible it says that "the soul of the life body" rests in the blood, so meat is made kosher by salting and soaking it, which draws out all the blood. Totally forbidden is the consumption of pork, hares, rabbits, and birds of prey. Storks, swallows, swans, and cuckoos are numbered among the latter. Forbidden, too, are crabs, crayfish, reptiles, oysters, insects, and especially carrion. The Jews slaughter animals according to rituals for which they have often been criticized. During the ritual slaughter a ritual slaughterer, the *shohet*, makes a sharp, quick cut across the animal's throat. This leads to an immediate blood vacuum in the brain, and the animal is stunned. No other kind of anesthesia is allowed. Any mistake during slaughtering, for example, if the animal isn't immediately stunned, means that it can't be processed any further. Jews don't mistreat animals. That reproach is as old as it is false. We don't have animal fights, cock fights, or bull fights. Battues as well as hunting with dogs are scorned. I don't know of any of our great men who hunted. In any case, the meat of an animal killed in a hunt is not kosher.

The devout Jew doesn't ask about the reasons for a law or any of the rules. He gladly accepts the "yoke of the law" as the will of God. I only want to talk about Judaism here insofar as it's necessary for understanding my life story. It's a world of its own, varied, and difficult to understand for an outsider, a world you could spend a lifetime studying without exhausting all the possibilities. Everything that I've talked about here is somehow connected with personal memories.

On the second day of Rosh Hashanah, the Danube Canal was always black with Orthodox Jews who traditionally wear a caftan, a hat, long beards, and the *peyot* or forelocks. The Orthodox Jews would pray aloud while swaying back and forth, a movement which is as integral to praying for Jews as folding hands is to Christians. They would throw bread crumbs into the water. The crumbs symbolize the sins that an Orthodox Jew has committed in the course of a year. Christians stood above on the quay and on the bridges and watched with either interest or disgust . . . Some yelled out names – no surprise since it's known that the Viennese like to call people names. At the beginning of the thirties, groups of Nazis would appear at *Tashlich* – the name of the ritual means "you shall cast away." . . . Anyway, in the early 1930s, groups of Nazis showed up in order to disrupt the event. The Orthodox Jews weren't used to defending themselves. They let themselves be pushed around, thrown into the water, and of course called names – mostly "Jewish swine." Soon thereafter, the police appeared, took up positions at the stairs leading down to the canal, and made sure that the Nazis didn't go down. It looked dangerous. Stones were thrown. The next year Jewish youth groups banded together to prevent the anti-Semites from attacking those praying.

In Vienna the Jewish community was comprised for the most part of Ashkenazim which more or less means "Germans," but includes Jews from all over Europe and the East with the exception of those from the Mediterranean countries. The Ashkenazim speak Yiddish. The Sephardim (Spaniards), Jews from the Mediterranean area, have different rituals and their language is Ladino. Ashkenazim and Sephardim usually don't intermarry.

I have particularly fond memories of Passover, the Jewish Easter celebration. Passover (passing over or sparing) lasts eight days. As described in the Bible, it gets its name from the time before the Exodus of the Jews when the Angel of Death passed over the Israelites' houses and spared them during the killing of the Egyptian first-born. The two evenings of the celebration, the Seder evenings (Seder means the order in which the ceremony takes place) proceed in the same fashion. The Haggadah, or the "telling," is read. It's the description of the Exodus of the Israelites from Egypt I already mentioned. The Haggadah, which, by the way, is the only illustrated religious work, contains popular songs which the family sings together. The final Seder song is known to every Jew, the song "One Baby Goat." "One baby goat, one baby goat which my father bought for two zuzeem. Then came a cat and devoured the baby goat, which my father bought for two zuzeem. Chad gad-yo, chad gad-yo, Then came a dog and bit the cat, which devoured the baby goat, which my father bought for two zuzeem . . ."

At last God himself appears and kills the Angel of Death who has killed the shohet, who slaughtered the ox, which drank the water, which extinguished the fire, which burned the staff, which beat the dog, which bit the cat, which devoured the baby goat, which my father bought for two zuzeem. Chad gad-yo, chad gad-yo.

The room is brightly lit, and the participants eat parsley and a potato that has been soaked in salt water, symbolizing the fruits of the earth as well as the tears the Israelites shed in Egyptian captivity. This is followed by a mixture made of pieces of apples and figs with nuts kneaded together using vinegar and seasoned with cinnamon. It ends up the color of the clay that "our ancestors had to work into bricks during forced labor." Next comes a boiled egg as a symbol of the variability and fragility of human destiny and a roasted bone with some meat on it as a symbol of the Passover lamb which the Israelites killed and ate before their Exodus from Egypt. Along with the other food only unleavened bread called *mazzah* is eaten for eight days. Because the Exodus from Egypt was made in such haste, the bread had to be baked before it could rise. And finally, a big goblet is filled with wine, whereupon a child goes to the door, opens it, and symbolically lets in the prophet Elijah. The goblet with wine for the prophet remains on the table during the entire celebration. On this evening all the guests – even the children – drink at least four glasses of raisin wine, which, by the way, doesn't harm anyone. People who live alone are also invited for the Seder evening. It's a very beautiful celebration, and I was secretly pleased that the prophet Elijah was among us.

I also remember Yom Kippur (the Day of Atonement) very well. On this day you try to make amends with yourself and the world, just as if you were about to die. Everyone thirteen and older fasts, starting in the evening and continuing until dark the next day, that is, until you can't tell a black thread from a white thread or until you see the first star. In the meantime you have to try to make peace with yourself and to ask the people you have wronged for forgiveness. No one is allowed to reject an apology. The sins committed against God will be forgiven, but not those committed against fellow humans. Yom Kippur is an important day. It's believed that incomplete remorse or half-hearted fasting can result in sickness, professional problems, or problems in love. The shofar, a ram's horn, is blown, calling on listeners to reflect and repent.

I have always looked forward to Sukkoth, which takes place five days later. Sukkoth is the Festival of the Tabernacles, commemorating the tentlike huts in which the Israelites lived during their trek through the desert. At the same time it celebrates the harvest. The huts are put up in the garden or on the balcony. They consist of boards and a roof of leaves through which you are supposed to see the stars. The symbol of the day is a festive bouquet consisting of *lulav* (palm branch), *hadasseh* (myrtle) and branches of a willow tree. In addition there is *etrog*, a citron.

Hanukkah, the Festival of Lights, is particularly popular with smaller children. Hanukkah means "dedication." When the Greek Antiochus Epiphanes conquered Palestine, he desecrated the Holy Temple in Jerusalem. The Maccabees, who recaptured it, rebuilt the altar on which a little pitcher with oil burned for eight days. In commemoration of the recorded event, the Hanukkah menorah is lit. Hanukkah is also celebrated at school. On each of the eight days one additional candle in the menorah is lit. The children receive little presents. At home they play with a dreidel, a little four-sided top made of wood. A Hebrew letter is etched onto each of the four sides of the top. Depending upon which side of the top is facing down when it falls, you have to put money into a kitty or you are allowed to take some out.

Purim is the Feast of Lots, commemorating the deliverance of the Jews in Persia from Haman, who was preparing an attack on them. In the Talmud there is only one commandment which demands Dionysian behavior: at the festival of Purim, believers are supposed to get so inebriated that they no longer know the difference between "Blessed be Mordechai," who was victorious over Haman, and "Cursed be Haman." It's said, "On Purim everything is allowed," and "Purim will outlast all celebrations." On Purim differences between rank and age don't count.

Everything is permitted, even the exchanging of men and women's clothing. In many ways the festival resembles Mardi gras. Special dishes are served: for example, the long *Haman's ears* made from noodle dough soaked in aniseed, or *kreplach* (meat-filled dumplings) for soup, or *hamantaschen* which are triangle-shaped poppyseed cakes filled with prunes.

The best-known symbols of Judaism are the Star of David and the menorah, the candelabrum at the Holy Temple with its seven branches. The yellow Star of David made of cloth was used by the Nazis to mark the Jews. It's a star with six corners, a hexagram formed by two equilateral triangles on top of one another. A menorah can be found in almost every Jewish household. However, true Judaism is contained in the Scriptures and is lived through faith. When the Romans destroyed the Temple of Jerusalem in the year 70 A.D., the Jews were dispersed to all corners of the earth. From that point on all lived in Diaspora or "exile." Wherever they ended up, they formed communities with a rabbi, if they were numerous enough. The spiritual center of the community was their faith, the Torah, and the Talmud. As soon as the community was big enough, they built a synagogue which is also called *shul* or temple. Synagogues are built facing east, in the direction of Jerusalem. In order to hold a service at least ten male worshippers or a *minyan* (number) have to be present. In the *heder* (room), the traditional Jewish elementary school in Eastern Europe, boys are taught from age four or five until their Bar Mitzvah, the Jewish "confirmation." This happens more often than not in a very unmethodical fashion and by private, uncertified teachers. The language Judaism is built on is Hebrew; children learn it at the Talmud Torah. As a result Jews carry their culture and religion within themselves. This leads to a certain separation from the cultures of other peoples with whom they live. At the same time they have often enough been segregated by others and put into ghettos. However, just as there is no unified Christianity, there is no unified Judaism.

The Jews have their own way of calculating time. The moon not the sun, determines the calendar. The year 1990 corresponds to

5750 in the Jewish calendar (which means it's the 5750th year after creation). The history of the Jewish religion is simultaneously the history of the Jews. Jews pray history, or so the saying goes.

School Days

I went to an elementary school on Kleine Sperlgasse. My mother went there too, just as my children did later on. A religion teacher instructed us twice a week in the precepts of the Jewish faith (and later, in high school, we had a teacher for religious instruction). In addition I went to the Talmud Torah in the Polish Synagogue for one or two hours in the afternoon. The Polish Synagogue was built in the Russian style and had an onion-shaped tower. There we read the Torah. On the right side of the book, the text was written in Hebrew, the German translation was on the left side. We had to cover up the German text with our left hand. After this, we read in Hebrew and translated into German. Our teacher, Rosenfeld, went through the class with a pointer: if you lifted your left hand in order to read the German text, he rapped you on the fingers or pulled your ears. There were about twenty of us. The parents of the richer students paid something for instruction. The poorer students, however, received it for free or were even given financial aid. The classroom was always "stuffed" full. (Of course there were only boys.) It was especially nice in the winter. The fire in the furnace crackled, and the atmosphere was very pleasant.

I often went with my grandfather to the Turkish Synagogue on Zirkusgasse – another house is currently being built where it once stood. The prayer room was richly decorated with Oriental ornaments, and in contrast to other synagogues it was quiet. That made a big impression on me.

The older I got, the more often I went to the amusement park, *Wurstl-Prater*. At that time the famous showman Calafati was still there. Little skits were performed in front of the booths to entice people to go in. Magicians performed . . . escape artists. I never entered any of the tents . . . I liked to listen to the beautiful music played in front of the tunnel of love. There I was first attracted to a girl, even though I didn't dare speak to her. I did, however, follow her on her way home. I lost her in the section of the city known as Erdberg. I was thirteen at the time. Most of the time I hung out in Leopoldstadt. Rarely did I ever go to another district. At that time unemployment and poverty were on the rise. For many years a Jewish beggar who played the violin and to whom we gave money stood on the Marien Bridge, across the Danube Canal. Most of the Jews in Leopoldstadt were anything but wealthy. The "rich" Jew is a myth . . . Of course he did exist, but he was the exception. My uncle, who had a stationer's store on Lilienbrunngasse, stacked up a "tower of pennies" beside the cash register like most of the Jewish shopkeepers. Beggars would come by and without saying a word would take two coins. They went from store to store. It had become such a tradition that they didn't even say "thank you" anymore. My uncle showed preference to beggars he knew personally (mostly either Jews or Social Democrats). For them he would set ten pennies aside. On Friday the door opened and closed constantly. The unemployed made music in the courtyards – with a violin, a guitar, or an accordion. They often sang along as they played. Residents would open their windows and throw down money wrapped in paper. Even before the Dollfuss era, SA troops roamed along the main avenue in the Prater, one of Vienna's largest parks, and beat up Jews who crossed their path. (The Dollfuss era from 1934 to 1938 was the time of the "corporate state." After the civil war in 1934, democracy was abolished and the Patriotic Front that grew out of the Christian Social movement ruled the state alone – Social Democrats, Communists, and National Socialists were outlawed.) I followed the SA troops out of curiosity, or even marched alongside them. Nobody bothered me because I wore short leather pants and a jacket in the style of the traditional costume, like all Viennese children. The children of Orthodox Jews who were dressed like their parents ran away. The SA invaded coffeehouses and outdoor restaurants and threw out anyone they didn't like. Already at age fourteen I thought to myself that we wouldn't be able to stay in Leopoldstadt much longer if things continued as they were. The SA often marched through Gredlergasse to Taborstraße. Their goal was the restaurant

Bayrischer Hof, the meeting place of the Viennese Nazis. Of course they intentionally chose a place in Leopoldstadt in order to provoke the Jewish residents. Today there's a chain store where the *Bayrischer Hof* once stood. After the war, when the place still existed, I was in the big hall once when the former Social Democratic Secretary of Interior Olah held a meeting there.

When the SA marched through Leopoldstadt, we looked out of the windows down to Schöllerhofgasse. I could hear the sounds of blows and screams coming from below on Blindengasse but couldn't see anything because it was already dark. The Nazis always came at dusk.

The SA sang loudly or screamed most of the time in unison "Germany, awake! Jew, croak!" I saw how they broke the windows of the grocer's on Gredlerstraße. Young Nazis preferred the weekend or night, and of course they always came in groups. They committed acts of terror as if it were their hobby. That was "good fun" for them, a great diversion. They almost always sang, "When Jewish blood drips from the knife, then things go twice as well." I watched this, as I said, from the window – also in the afternoon. The fights, however, took place only after it got dark. When the Patriotic Front came to power in 1934 the incidents stopped, but in 1938 they resumed in full force. However, even during the time of the "corporate state" tensions existed. At school it was generally known which teachers were illegal Nazis. In elementary school almost all the students were Jewish, and we had an easygoing non-Jewish teacher named Hugo Hahn who came from the Forest District. Later, during the Nazi period, when Jews were being locked in the elementary school before deportation, he protested how inhumane it was that they had to stand packed in the rooms without food and water. As punishment he was drafted, but he survived. After the war I visited him together with my mother. He was very moved and cried because he had believed that I had been killed like most of the others.

In junior high school on Kleine Sperlgasse more than three-quarters of the students were Jewish. Some of the teachers were Jewish, some Christian. The physical education teachers were for

the most part Nazis. One of them wore a green hat and
knickerbockers. He was particularly unfriendly and nasty. I have
no fond memories of physical education. The teachers who were
illegal Nazis taught us only because they were happy to have a job
at all. My natural science teacher, however, quit, since he didn't
want to teach at a school where, as he said, almost all of the
students were Jews. I was sorry to see him go since I enjoyed his
lectures. Most of the Jewish teachers who taught us were Social
Democrats.

After junior high school, at age fourteen, I went to the
technical high school in the Arsenal – formerly one of the royal
and imperial barracks on the edge of town. In contrast to junior
high there were few Jewish students and only one Jewish teacher,
a Mr. Pollack who taught electrical engineering. With the
exception of one or two children, the non-Jewish students had Nazi
parents and also behaved like little Nazis. Of course, they were
anti-Semitic. The children of Social Democrats were the rare
exception. Many children from rural areas, especially from the
Forest District, attended school at the Arsenal. They particularly
liked to hassle the Jewish students. Either they imitated the way
the Orthodox Jews spoke and ridiculed their behavior or they
"accidentally" bumped into them. During recess the Jewish
students always stood together in a corner as a means to protect
themselves. Although nobody was openly beaten, it was obvious
that we weren't welcome. This didn't bother the Orthodox Jews
much, because they had a different attitude owing to their faith, but
I suffered very much. I considered myself Austrian. By the way,
our class consisted of thirty students. Altogether there were five
Orthodox Jews. They weren't allowed to carry anything on
Saturday, the Sabbath, not even a book-bag. What is more, their
religion forbade them from taking notes on this day. In addition to
myself, there were three other "assimilated" Jewish students whose
religious upbringing was either not as strict or nonexistent. Friday
after school the Orthodox students left their book-bags at school;
thus they didn't have to bring them on Saturday. During class
others took notes for them or lent them their notebooks over the

weekend. After school I always carried two or three book-bags to the Marien Bridge. We walked because the Orthodox Jews were also not allowed to take the streetcar on the Sabbath. After we crossed over the Marien Bridge to the Leopoldstadt side of the bridge, they carried their book-bags themselves – the Sabbath laws allowed them to do that since Leopoldstadt is an island. There is also the Sabbath law that you may not walk more than 2000 meters beyond a settled area, so if our school took a field trip on the weekend, the Orthodox students went along for two kilometers and then sat down on a bench and had a snack. In this manner they had reached a "new" locality and were then allowed to go another two kilometers. This elicited amazement and ridicule from the other students. I soon became friends with the Orthodox students because they were treated with such a lack of understanding. However, I didn't become any more religious because of it. Just the opposite happened. I gradually lost my faith.

I was an average student, but I always was promoted to the next grade without problems. At that time, the *Matura* – the high school exit and college entrance examination – didn't exist yet; it was introduced under Hitler.

The Socialist Pittermann, who was later to become vice-chancellor, was our teacher in history, German, and geography. He always protected the Jewish students. I can remember that he recited the Styrian author Peter Rosegger in dialect.

The political leanings of each teacher were known . . . There were also illegal Nazis among them – the so-called "thousand percent" Nazis – those who didn't even try to hide the fact that they were Nazis. Even if they had tried, their rhetoric would have given them away. However, they never confronted us directly with their views. At the end of the fifties, I ran into the math teacher. He still was a Nazi and an anti-Semite. He invited me to the Café Ministerium on the Stubenring. After the war he had been transferred to Mödling, and he complained how badly he was being treated in the new democratic state and he carried on about the Jews – I don't know what he was thinking.

But there were also others. For example, there was Emma

Holbek, a married maid who worked for my grandmother. She was a Czech Catholic who was twenty years old at that time. At Christmas time she invited me to her home and showed me the big Christmas tree. (My family was never hostile towards Catholics.) From 1938 until my grandmother's deportation, Emma Holbek shopped for her and helped out with food. The caretaker in my parent's building, Fritz Wessely, was actually a streetcar worker and his wife did the custodial work in the building. Wessely was a member of the *Schutzbund*. (The *Schutzbund* or "Protective League" was the militia of the Social Democrats.) When the Nazis came to get the Jews in 1938 and 1939, he locked the main entrance and didn't let anybody in.

1934

February 12, 1934, was the decisive turning point. All of a sudden, during mechanical engineering class, the lights went out. Our teacher advised us to run straight home. On my way home I noticed that none of the streetcars were running. Only later when we turned on the radio did we find out what had happened. The workers were involved in fights with the police and the army. I believed democratic socialism to be a just cause; its goal was a society free of capitalism. For me it contained the solution to the Jewish question. By virtue of the fact that all people would be regarded as equal, I thought that problems between Christians and Jews would disappear. I equated socialism with progress: community housing, new parks, public swimming pools, and adult education centers were built at that time − all that impressed me. For that reason my first reaction to the news from the radio was joy. The Social Democrats had been oppressed anyway. Their arsenals had been emptied and they had been attacked in the newspapers. But then the news got progressively worse. The next day the electricity had been turned on again, and the streetcars were also running. From that we concluded that the proclaimed general strike hadn't been observed by all the rank and file. Two days later, while looking out the window on Gredlerstraße, I saw the police leading through the streets groups of thirty to forty arrested workers, who either held their hands behind their heads or were tied up. There had been two resistance groups in our district on Ausstellungsstraße. We didn't go to school for two or three days. On February 13 the streetcars had started running again, and I realized by then, that the cause had been lost. From that day on I ceased considering myself an Austrian. It was clear to me then that I was a Jew, and I began to accept it.

The Social Democratic party was outlawed, just as the Communists and the Nazis had been, by the way. With the institution of the Patriotic Front, Dollfuss announced the founding of the "corporate state." Today the years 1934-1938 are referred to as "Austro-fascism." In 1934, after four days of civil war, we were deeply depressed when we heard about the executions — Koloman Wallisch in Styria and the engineer Weissl in Vienna. Engelbert Dollfuss stayed in power until his assassination by the Nazis. He was followed by Schuschnigg who was head of state until Hitler marched into Austria. Neither of them, however, persecuted the Jews (on the contrary). There were hardly any followers of Dollfuss among the teachers at school anymore. With the exception of one or two who remained Social Democrats, all had become Nazis. The students were instructed to wear a badge. It showed a red triangle with the inscription: "Stand united." During the entire Dollfuss era we knew that this state couldn't last. On the one hand, we were glad that it existed because the National Socialists were outlawed and the attacks on the Jews in Leopoldstadt had stopped; on the other hand, whenever we took trips into outlying areas, we could see that the movement lived on. Big white swastikas had been painted on rocks.

The *Shomer Hazair*

Although my teachers and fellow students continued to behave as they had previously, I was sobered by the experience. As long the Social Democrats had been around, I had hoped they would come to power. At this point I saw no future for me in Austria. The Association of Socialist High School Students of which I was a member had been disbanded and so, at the age of sixteen, I joined the *Shomer Hazair* (the Young Guard), a Zionist youth organization ideologically to the left of the Social Democrats. It was a select movement in favor of a bi-national Jewish state with the Arabs. It wanted to abolish capitalism, and it developed the idea of the kibbutz movement. In fact later, as the Mapam party, it did pioneering work in Israel. You could say its orientation is atheistic. I joined the *Shomer Hazair* – which, by the way, exists all over the world, having been founded in Vienna during the early twenties by Jews from Galicia – in the year of 1934. It was in this year, after I stopped considering myself an Austrian, that I decided to emigrate to Palestine, but first I wanted to finish school. It was difficult to get to Israel. Most of the time the immigrants got there illegally by way of Turkey and Syria. As a rule only a limited number of immigration certificates were issued. In order to get one you had to put your name on long waiting lists.

Every Friday evening the members of the *Shomer Hazair* met on Haasgasse, later on Kleine Pfarrgasse. The meeting place – a room in a cellar – was lit with candles because of the Sabbath. Most of the time Hebrew songs were played by a band. Religious holidays were celebrated as if they were national holidays; it was all very easygoing. We wore blue shirts like the *Rote Falken* (Red Falcons), the youth organization of the Socialists. The *Shomer Hazair* shaped me for decades to come. It was tolerated by the state because we weren't involved in Austrian politics, but instead we intended to emigrate to Palestine. Only then did I slowly become religious again, since I realized that the *Shomer* was only standing on *one* leg – but we Jews had to stand on both.

Every Sunday, the *Shomer* – boys and girls together – took trips to the Vienna Woods. The youngest in the group were affectionately called "Benjamin," and the group included students from elementary school up to fourteen years old.

The *Shomer* rejected "assimilation," and I, for my part, gradually stopped wishing to be accepted as an Austrian. Of course another goal was to liberate the Jews from their ghettoized existence. We didn't drink or smoke and we neither went to coffeehouses nor took dancing lessons. The closest comparison to us might be the German youth organization the *Wandervögel* (Wandering Birds). We sat around the campfire and sang, or we met at the youth center. There were also other Jewish organizations like the *Betar*,[1] the movement of Jabotinsky. The members wore brown shirts; they were nationalistic Zionists, anti-Socialist, and militant. We called them Fascist, they called us Communist. During trips fights with them often broke out, but I always avoided fights. The *Benei Akiba*,[2] the youth movement of the *Misrachi* (east), had a religious Zionist orientation, and rabbis were in charge there. Other organizations were more moderate and without set goals. In blue and white cans, we collected money which was used to buy land in Palestine. Jabotinsky, in contrast, took the view that land couldn't be bought, but only won with blood – thus the militant training at the *Betar*.

Lizzy Weiser

At the *Shomer* everyone received a Hebrew name. I was called Seef (Wolf) instead of Karl. In 1935 I met Lizzy Weiser at the *Shomer*; she was two years younger than I was. At the *Shomer* she was called Alisa (The Cheerful One). Her parents were assimilated Jews and lived at the edge of the Vienna Prater in an exclusive residential district called *Schüttel*. Her father, Rudolf Weiser, a high official of the federal railway, was a handsome man. He painted pictures in his free time. He often invited me over. Later I felt very comfortable at Lizzy's parents' because it was never as tense there as at home. Lizzy was a pretty girl with blue eyes and ash blond hair. She wore dirndls, the fashion at that time. Today one would say she was a typical Viennese girl. She knew nothing about Judaism, by the way. I was very much in love with her. At first I kept the relationship a secret from my parents, but when I told them everything, they visited Lizzy's parents and invited them to our home. (The stronger the National Socialists got in Germany,

---

[1] Named after a fortified city to the west of Jerusalem.
[2] Named after a popular figure of Talmudic Judaism.

the closer the Jews moved together. Differences that had earlier seemed so important now were viewed as inconsequential. For assimilated Jews, Judaism was often something unpleasant, something you actually didn't like to be associated with. Now they started to see it in a different light.)

Lizzy's parents and mine soon suspected and knew that it would be necessary to emigrate. In 1934 all Jews were very sorry that Chancellor Dollfuss had been assassinated by the Nazis. All over Vienna the Catholics put candles in the windows – because of his assassination Dollfuss became more popular in Austria than he had ever been when he was alive. However, the *Heimwehr* (home army), the militia on the side of the Patriotic Front, and their commanders Fey and Starhemberg were still despised. As I mentioned, unemployment was very high. For Jews especially it became harder and harder to find work. Business was going badly, and Jewish companies didn't dare employ Jews because it would have stirred up the already anti-Semitic population. What followed was the dismissal of many Jews – first the college graduates, then the white-collar workers. After I graduated from high school, I didn't find work in Vienna until four weeks before I fled. Then I started as a trainee on Berggasse – in the warehouse of a textile company owned by Jews.

I always looked forward to the weekends. Every Saturday afternoon I worked as a claqueur at the Volkstheater and had to applaud loudly in exchange for free tickets. From time to time Lizzy and I went to the Rembrandt, the Augarten, or the Helios movie theaters. The *Shomer*, however, didn't approve if you went your own way. Life was supposed to take place within the group.

After the evening social gatherings at the youth center, I walked Lizzy home through the Prater for half an hour. For a long time we had a very innocent relationship. We were both inexperienced in love. When we said goodnight it was usually no later than ten o'clock.

In my leisure time I liked to play ping-pong. On Taborstraße, where the Hotel Zentral is now located, there was a table-tennis hall with eight tables that belonged to a Jew, Mr. Flußmann. You had to pay a small sum for the use of the table, the paddles, and the ball. Once I played Bergmann, the European champion. Of course he was much better than I was. Aside from that I read a lot. Most of the books I read I had to borrow, because I only owned three books: *The Three Musketeers* by Alexander Dumas, *Oliver Twist* by Charles Dickens, and *Les Miserables* by Victor Hugo. As a child I read *Rübezahl* and *Max and Moritz*, *Robinson Crusoe*, *Gulliver's Travels*, the *Legends of Classical Antiquity*, *Germanic Heroic Sagas*, and *Sigismund Rüstig*, the story of a stranded sailor. In addition I went swimming regularly – in winter in Diana Pool, in summer at *Gänsehäufel*, a beach along one of the arms of the Danube.

Then, in 1938, my life changed abruptly.

1938 – The Anschluss

We expected Chancellor Schuschnigg, the successor to the assassinated Dollfuss, to be more moderate than his predecessor. But we were sadly mistaken.

Hardship was widespread, also among the Jews. Because of this I didn't understand the anti-Semitism that resulted from the unemployment. To be sure, there were many Jewish doctors and lawyers in Vienna and many small Jewish stores, but in Leopold-stadt the majority could barely make ends meet, if even that.

The National Socialist movement became such an elemental force, first in Germany, then also in Austria (during its period of illegality), that it seemed inexorable. Youth and workers in particular were drawn to it.

On February 12 Schuschnigg and Hitler met at Obersalzberg; as a result Schuschnigg was forced to include Seyss-Inquart as Secretary of Interior in his government. We considered that a bad omen. Two weeks later Schuschnigg met with a delegation of illegal Social Democrats who offered him their support against the Nazis, but Schuschnigg didn't make any promises. Before the invasion of the German troops on March 12, one could see the *Kruckenkreuze*, the crossed-shaped symbols of the corporate state, painted all over the pavement and on buildings. There was no visible counter-propaganda on the part of the Nazis, who were still formally illegal. The Christian Socials handed out leaflets in Vienna calling for a "free, Christian, German Austria." There were demonstrations, members of the *Heimwehr* came in uniform from the provinces and held parades. All of a sudden – two or three days before the invasion by the German troops – the Social Democrats resurfaced. They came mostly from the working class districts and demonstrated for Austria. In the evenings until March 11 demonstrations by both Nazis and anti-Nazis took place simultaneously on Roten-Turm-Straße: on one side the demonstrators would yell "Heil Schuschnigg," on the other side their adversaries would yell "Heil Hitler." Socialists and Communists also demonstrated for Austria. Clenched fists were raised. I

marched on the side for Austria, but I never joined in the
screaming. The police kept the crowds apart – otherwise fighting
would have broken out. Suddenly – right before the German army
marched in – it became known that Schuschnigg had resigned . . .
After that the Christian Socials and the Social Democrats fled into
the side streets in droves and the Nazis ruled the streets. Jubilant
cries erupted: "Sieg Heil" and "Germany, awake!" Suddenly a
group of policemen wearing armbands with swastikas appeared.
An unbelievable flush of victory came over the people. I hurried
home . . . The Jews hardly dared to go out anymore, . . . not even
in Leopoldstadt.

Jews Have to Scrub the Streets

Hitler marched into Vienna shortly thereafter, on March 14.
Flags with the swastika hung everywhere, on buildings and from
windows. The streets were crowded with people. Right after the
proclamation on Heldenplatz, where Hitler had spoken to the
crowd from the balcony of the *Hofburg*, the former imperial residence, Jews had to wash the *Kruckenkreuze* from the pavement and
the walls. Unable to stay at home, I went downtown. I don't look
particularly Jewish and was wearing leather shorts. When I passed
beyond the Sweden Bridge, I saw a crowd forming. I approached
it and saw that the passersby had formed a circle. Jewish men and
women, some men dressed in caftans, others in normal street
clothes, were kneeling in the middle of the circle and were busy
scrubbing the *Kruckenkreuze* with a lye solution and brushes. They
were accompanied by gloating catcalls from the people encircling
them. Pedestrians who looked Jewish were also pushed into the
circle and forced to "work along." The spectators considered this
"great fun." There wasn't a policeman in sight, but there were
uniformed men wearing armbands with swastikas on them. You
could hear insults being hurled. I didn't dare contradict them.
Passersby who were revolted by what was going on looked away
and hurried on. On the one hand, I wasn't afraid since nobody paid
attention to me; on the other hand, I didn't dare move on because
I was afraid I would attract attention to myself. When everything

had been washed away, the Jews had to line up and the crowd dispersed. I too walked on. On my way I saw other groups who were scrubbing down walls. I didn't stop anymore, but sneaked home through side streets. This popular form of "amusement" went on for a few days. On the way to my grandmother's I saw Nazis pull Jews out of coffeehouses and drive them away on trucks for interrogation. In the process they were shoved around and insulted. The Jews consented to everything. What else could they have done? Of course I also saw that the shutters and shop windows in Leo‑ poldstadt were smeared with the word Jew and the Star of David.

What Came Next

On April 10 a plebiscite was supposed to be held concerning the Anschluss which had taken place. The Bishop's Council composed a pastoral letter which recommended a yes vote at the plebiscite. Cardinal Innitzer signed it with "Heil Hitler." Writing in the Viennese newspaper *Neues Wiener Tageblatt*, the future Austrian president, Social Democrat Karl Renner also supported a union with Nazi Germany. Meanwhile, Hermann Goering had declared at a rally that Vienna had to be "purged of Jews" within four years.

On to Slovakia

At this time I applied at the Czech Consulate for a passport because I wanted to leave Vienna and look for work in Slovakia. At the consulate I was informed that I no longer had to serve in the Czech army because it was a lost cause. I was advised to emigrate to England because visas between England and Czechoslovakia were not required. Later I remembered this advice. I registered with the *Shomer* for emigration to Palestine and said good-bye to Lizzy. Lizzy went to Schwardorf in Marchfeld – the flat farmland area east of Vienna along the March River. On the estate of a Jew, youths from the *Shomer* were introduced to farm work. I had no great desire to go to that estate. I wasn't interested in farm work and I had relatives in Slovakia: my father's brother and sister and their families. Actually, it was an escape. I wanted to leave Vienna, and Czechoslovakia was still democratic.

Zilina

My knowledge of the Slovakian language was very minimal. I worked as an assistant lathe hand in a little factory in Zilina that produced narrow-gauge railways for mines. A German migrant worker, who happened not to be a Nazi, taught me a lot about the trade. The factory belonged to a Hungarian Jew, Arpad Stark. His hiring me was interpreted as favoritism. Here, too, darkness was descending. A few months later, on September 29, Hitler, Chamberlain, Daladier, and Mussolini signed the Treaty of Munich which provided for the surrender of border areas of Czechoslovakia to the German Reich. Half a year later Hitler occupied the rest of the country. From the time I worked in Zilina up until the Munich Treaty I was very unhappy.

My aunt Irene Ring owned a profitable shoestore on the main square, which she managed together with her husband Jakob. She had two daughters, Magda and Lydia. Since the family, with the exception of Magda, was generally unfriendly and behaved in an arrogant way, I lived with them for only a few days. They were against the *Shomer*, which in their eyes was made up solely of Communists. The apartment was above the store on the beautiful main square that had a colonnade under which farmers sold strawberries and blueberries.

After a short time I moved in with my uncle Heinrich Berger, his wife, and their daughter. My uncle Heinrich was a Socialist and worked as typesetter for a newspaper. My aunt's views, on the other hand, were conservative, but she wasn't Orthodox (in the religious sense). Both were poor. Before Hitler they often came to Vienna to visit my father, who gave them money. Uncle Heinrich was not very respected within the family because he was only a worker and not a merchant. He took me in with open arms. The street where I lived was located between two cemeteries. I paid for room and board and spent my free time at the *Shomer*.

The people in Zilina had no idea what was happening in Austria. They didn't know that Jews had lost their jobs and that their stores had been expropriated. At that time I myself couldn't imagine the extermination of the Jews, although anti-Semitism was also noticeable in Slovakia. For example, on the walls of the buildings you could see the words "ZIDA DO PALESTINY" and "NA SLOVENSKU LEN SLOVA'CI" – "Jews to Palestine" and "Slovakia for Slovaks." But the pressure put on the Jews there wasn't as great as it was in Vienna. They were still allowed to keep their stores and factories. However, the nationalists didn't like to hear German spoken in Slovakia, and the state was very nationalistically oriented.

Indeed, as became clear later, it was very fortunate for me that I left Zilina again. With great certainty I would have been killed in Slovakia if I hadn't been able to emigrate to England. In Vienna the situation had gotten progressively worse. My grandmother's apartment had been expropriated as well as my uncle Elias' stationer's store. They had no income anymore and lived off their meager savings. Together with other Jewish families they were crowded into an apartment in a building on Karmelitermarkt. Jews from all over the district were packed into this building. In desperation some threw themselves out the window. My grandmother and uncle lived there for a few months, then they were taken to our elementary school, where they finally were deported. Neither of them returned.

Vienna

As soon as Lizzy had returned from Schwardorf to Vienna, I traveled by ship on the Danube from Zilina to Vienna. In contrast to my grandmother and uncle, my father was allowed to keep our apartment because he was a Czech citizen. Standing in front of the door, I saw the sign: "This apartment is under the protection of the Czech General Consulate." Most of the other tenants had been forced to move to the building on Karmelitermarkt or had emigrated. The emigrants had "sold" their furniture. "Illegal Nazis" who had joined the party before the troops marched in or Nazis who had connections with higher-ups in the party had moved into the "unoccupied" apartments. Previously only Jews had lived in our building, but now – with the exception of my parents – only one Austrian remained from all the Jewish tenants. She was a widow who had been married to a Jew in a mixed marriage.

A dress code was also issued, which prohibited Jews from wearing white stockings and leather shorts. Benches in the park had signs that read: "Not for Jews." We were also not allowed to swim at Diana Pool, only in Roman Pool, which was frequented exclusively by Jews. The soccer club *Hakoah* was disbanded. An immense process of disintegration was taking place among the Jews in Vienna. I had barely arrived in Vienna when I wanted to leave again. Of course I couldn't find work anywhere, so I decided to emigrate to Palestine with Lizzy. We discussed it whenever we met and imagined our future in Palestine, which made us feel optimistic. The *Shomer* still existed. It had moved to a building on Tempelgasse, and most of the time we met there and studied Hebrew.

My Father

My father was fifty at that time and spoke neither English nor Hebrew. He didn't know where to emigrate or what to do. He only wanted my sister and me to leave the country. My mother, on the other hand, didn't want to leave without my grandmother, the two of them being very close.

Miklos

Finally, in 1940, my family emigrated to Slovakia, to Miklos, where my father had been born and where there were numerous leather factories. I had been there often as a child. The Waag River ran through the village, and from the bridge you could watch the leather floating by. The terrible odor could be smelled throughout the village. Rich Jewish leather factory owners lived in Miklos, but my father was poorly treated. I know he was very disappointed.

Hechaluz

After my return I applied for a certificate of emigration for Palestine together with Lizzy. The office that issued these certificates was located on Salzgries and was called *Hechaluz* (The Pioneer). We waited in vain. In the meantime the members of the Betar tried to escape by ship on the Danube.

Kristallnacht

Kristallnacht was a pogrom against Jews organized by the National Socialists. It took place on the night of November 9. Although there was no need for an additional incentive, this event reinforced the desire to emigrate. Using Herschel Grünspan's assassination of the German diplomat Ernst von Rath in Paris as a pretext, the Nazis portrayed the riots as acts of spontaneous outrage. I heard about the assassination on the radio. In the evening, I watched from the window as SS men ran into Leopoldstadt. I was afraid and didn't leave the house. Our caretaker had again locked the door to the building. Suddenly word spread that the synagogues were burning. Wanting to see that at all costs, I ran into the street. Perhaps I was naive, because I didn't consider the danger I put myself in. On Karmelitermarkt and Schiffgasse groups of people were standing on the sidewalks. The curious ones who watched the fire cursed the Jews, and the few Jews whom I encountered were dismayed. The Schiff Shul was in flames. Although the general mood was charged with hatred, I wasn't accosted. That didn't surprise me, though, since most of the time I wasn't taken for a Jew. Once I was even stopped on the Aspern Bridge by a man with a collection box who asked for a donation for the German Winter Assistance. I gave him a coin in order not to raise suspicion and the man pinned a little carved man on my lapel. Strangely enough, I can only remember a few details about the *Kristallnacht*; however, I can still see the burning Schiff Shul collapse before my eyes.

Escape

Girls and younger women had the possibility of working as domestic help in England, although they had to find families who would take them in. There were many Jewish and non-Jewish families in England who were willing to do that even if they didn't

really need help. Lizzy didn't know anything about domestic work
or child-rearing, but her parents considered this a possibility to get
her away in time and unharmed. Leaving the country was difficult.
Lizzy had to stand in line at the British Consulate for days and had
to prove that she didn't have any debts. A large line had formed in
front of the building. When she finally was given an entrance
permit and a work permit, we went to West Station. I still can
remember that our parents, who also paid for the traveling
expenses, accompanied us up to the platform. What is more, my
father gave me ten marks to take along in case of an emergency. I
saw him for the last time on that platform. He waved at me as the
train started to move. My sister Ditta and my mother had also
come.

Only women who were going to England sat in the train car.
As far as I can remember, they were all Jews. Nobody spoke until
we reached the border. All were preoccupied by the fear of being
stopped and sent back.

I was wearing shorts and a trench coat. My drafting
instruments and my textbook for mechanical engineering by
Freytag were in my luggage. I had the feeling that I would never
return to Vienna . . . Everything had happened in such a rush . . .
Actually, I was glad to be sitting on the train. I hadn't cried when
saying good-bye. After all, I was with my girlfriend Lizzy, even if
the situation of my parents and sister troubled me. I had a suitcase
with underclothing and one sweater and, of course, my Czech
passport. In Vienna I had heard that travelers leaving the country
with a Czech passport were stopped at the border and taken from
the train. After that they were taken to Dachau. Dachau was
already known as a symbol for the Nazi terror. Therefore, I was
very much afraid of the border guards. In Cologne I bought a little
bottle of cologne on the platform (I don't know why I remember
that). Lizzy cried during the entire trip. She had started to cry when
she said good-bye to her parents at West Station. We finally
reached the Dutch border and I was asked what I had with me. I
answered, "Ten marks and the ring I have on my finger." The
border guard returned the passport and said, "Let's leave well

enough alone." He didn't even search my suitcase. I was glad to leave Germany behind me, though I secretly feared that the Dutch could give us trouble. But they only asked us our destination, and we were allowed to pass through. Although mixed with sadness, the atmosphere in the compartment was suddenly relaxed when we traveled through Holland. We had all left our relatives behind and faced an uncertain future. For the first time during the trip we struck up a conversation. Everyone told where they came from and how they spent the last days before their escape. We reached the port of Veissingen in the afternoon and boarded an English ship named the *Vindobona*. For me it was the supreme irony that, of all things, it was named after the city I had left behind. Moreover, in one of the ship's gangways I discovered an old etching of Vienna with St. Stephan's Cathedral on it. That struck me as very peculiar.

Arrival

We docked at Harwich, and I waited to see what would happen. There was a separate gangway leading to the border guard for English passengers. I stood on board and envied them for being English. Lizzy was ahead of me; she had the permit-stamp in her passport and was allowed on shore. Then I was asked why I wanted to enter England. I passed myself off as a tourist and started to stammer. My English was not very good at the time. In addition I was nervous. At that point the immigration officer wanted to know how much money I had on me. I declared, "Ten marks."

"That won't get you far . . .," the officer said. "Do you want to visit someone?"

I replied, "I don't have anyone."

In front of the ship a train was waiting which Lizzy had boarded in the meantime. I didn't panic since I knew her address, but it was an unpleasant situation.

"I can't let you in," said the official. "You are a refugee not a tourist. Remember, when you come to England you always have to tell the truth." He then sent me back to the ship. From the deck I could see the train that Lizzy had boarded depart. The ship was supposed to dock at Veissingen the next day and I knew if nothing happened, the Dutch would send me back to Germany. On board nobody paid attention to me. I sat down in front of the etching of Vienna and waited. It was nauseating. All night long I was in low spirits and I couldn't sleep a wink. The next morning, when the crew prepared to cast off, an English officer approached me and instructed me to go ashore. I was taken to a building with a waiting room. In the meantime the *Vindobona* took off. However, they intended – as I found out later – to send me back on another ship. Around noon Lizzy called from London and calmed me down. She had been at the Jewish Refugee Committee, and they had promised her that they would issue a guarantee that I wouldn't be a burden to the country. In England, too, there was unemployment. I went back to the waiting room where I was alone with my thoughts and fears. In the afternoon Lizzy appeared with a lady called Allison Wood, a Quaker from a distinguished family who did volunteer work for the Jewish Refugee Committee. The Quakers did a lot for the refugees during World War II. Mrs. Wood brought me an affidavit which I presented to the officials who had wanted to send me back. The official was very friendly, checked the papers, and stamped the following into my passport: "Permitted to land and to stay in Great Britain for six months under the condition that the holder does not take any employment paid or unpaid." That meant that I had to be supported by the committee. We took the next train to London, which was packed with refugees. We left without knowing where I would sleep that night.

In London

A man with a Star of David on his jacket was waiting for us on the platform in London. It was already late and dark. He spoke to us in a mixture of English and Yiddish which I could hardly understand. Finally I had to say good-bye to Lizzy.

We went to the Jewish Shelter, a miserable hostel with a large dormitory room. Men lay in bed watching the new arrivals. After I had stowed away my luggage, I was given something to eat, but I was just repulsed and horrified by everything I saw. The hostel managers were extremely unfriendly to me. They were used to receiving Eastern European Jews who had escaped from Poland, Russia, and Rumania, and who spoke Yiddish. If you didn't speak Yiddish, as was the case with me, they didn't consider you a real Jew anymore, but a goy, a stranger. I didn't like the food which consisted of pickled herring and bread. Very early the next morning I left the Jewish Shelter. At Whitechapel Road I got into one of the double-decker busses, although I had no idea where it was going. I just looked at the shop windows without buying anything. Lizzy had given me a few shillings, but I wanted to save them for a snack or a place to stay. In the evening I sought out the Salvation Army on Whitechapel Road. The conditions there were even worse than in the Jewish Shelter. The dormitory room was a large room like the nave of a church. Over a hundred iron bed-frames were lined up in it . . . I was among the homeless, hobos, and beggars. Soon I found out that the sheets were full of fleas . . . The Salvation Army was a large night shelter. The next day I returned to the Jewish Shelter; from there I was sent to the committee, together with another refugee.

In the Country

The Refugee Committee was working together with Dorman's Land, a beautiful estate with a castlelike villa and splendid gardens an hour outside of London. We weren't allowed to stay at Dorman's Land, however, but were assigned to an affiliated estate, Old Surrey Hall at Apsley Town. There we had to do a variety of jobs, as either groundskeepers, lumberjacks, or farm workers. Old Surrey Hall had been turned into a sort of refugee camp. I met many refugees – we were thirty-eight young men who all shared a similar fate. We were allowed to go for walks, but we couldn't leave the grounds. Since there was very little to eat, I was always hungry. Most of the time I worked in the woods using a horse-drawn cart. We sawed tree trunks, loaded them, and burned the branches. I wrote my parents that I was doing well, in order not to worry them. After having been there two weeks, I called Lizzy, and two weeks later she came to Apsley Town for a visit. We took a walk in the woods and had a lot to talk about. I wasn't allowed to take her to my room, which I shared with another man.

Tomaschov

I stayed at the camp until the beginning of the war and Lizzy visited me every weekend she had off. I couldn't afford a train ticket (we only received a little pocket money, just enough for a few cigarettes). Otherwise nothing would have kept me from going to London. After a while I became friends with another emigrant from Bratislava (Pressburg) who was the same age. His name was Tomaschov. He came from a well-known Orthodox family. The first thing we had in common was that he wasn't a German . . . With our Czech passports we were the only "friendly aliens" in the camp. "Friendly aliens" were refugees who didn't come from Germany or Austria, in contrast to the "enemy aliens." The "enemy aliens" had to testify before tribunals which decided if they should be detained or not.

Joining the Military

We suffered most from the fact that we couldn't envision a future. When I heard on the radio one day that England was at war with Germany, I was very happy. Finally some action was being taken against Hitler, who was getting stronger and stronger in Europe. I decided to go to London on my own and enlist in the army. At the next best opportunity I stopped a car on the road and asked to be taken along. When the driver heard that I wanted to join the military, he was very willing to help. An atmosphere of change had seized the entire country. In London I reported to the Jewish Committee and let them know that I was going to enlist. The Jewish Committee was hardly pleased by it. Moreover, Mrs. Allison Wood, the Quaker who was in charge of my case, was against the war for religious reasons. She advised me to enroll in a class for welders and to work in the war industry. However, I reported to the Czech Consulate, where my offer was gratefully accepted, even though it was made clear to me that some time would go by before a legion would be established. (Today I think that the older refugees were smarter. They worked, earned money in order to buy a house one day. We, the younger ones, enlisted in the army instead.) I returned to the farm and conferred with Tomaschov about what we should do. We didn't want to stay in Apsley Town when there was a war on and history was being made.

Lizzy's Parents

In the meantime Lizzy's parents had escaped from Austria. I met them in Hyde Park during my trip to London. They had only gotten a permit to stay because they wanted to emigrate to Chicago. There were quotas for immigrants to America. The Americans agreed to take in a set number of refugees if someone vouched for them. This voucher, the so-called affidavit, was usually provided by relatives or rich Jews like the Lauder family who vouched for many Jewish refugees, saving many lives. Lizzy's parents had affidavits and received visas too. In Vienna I had also tried to emigrate to America. And it's true, I had received an affidavit, but the quota for Czech Jews was significantly lower than that for German Jews. I would have had to wait for two years before being able to emigrate, or so I was told in Vienna. In the face of the coming events this wouldn't have been possible.

I first assumed that Lizzy's parents would go in advance, but at our meeting her father presented me with the fait accompli that Lizzy had to accompany him to America. He believed that a temporary separation might be good; we would see if we really belonged together. We were still very young and we shouldn't rush things. I was twenty years old at that time and Lizzy nineteen. I said` "Fine, but let us get married beforehand." Lizzy wanted to get married, too, but she was very attached to her father. I couldn't change his mind. And his wife did whatever he wanted her to do.

Good-byes

On the day of her departure, I accompanied Lizzy to King's Cross Station, where the trains left for Bristol. Engines with steam pouring out of them stood on the tracks. Lizzy's parents boarded one of the trains so we could be alone to say good-bye to each other. We took a walk on the platform. Lizzy gave me her address, then she had to get into the compartment with her parents. I remember how the piston rod and the wheels of the engine started to move. Lizzy wept. I can't cry in such situations. I felt very lonely and abandoned as the train slowly disappeared from the station.

1940 My Plan

From then on I didn't want to remain on the farm under any circumstances. I intended to find a ship and follow Lizzy to America. Tomaschov hesitated, but in the end we left the camp without giving notice. We did have Czech passports and hoped to be permitted to move about freely because of them.

On to Plymouth

In London we immediately looked up the employment offices at the harbor. There we were rejected, however, because of the stipulation that only Englishmen were allowed to work on English ships. We were told that it would be easier to get on a ship in Plymouth. During the war it was relatively easy to hitch a ride. Out of goodwill, people often drove us an hour out of their way. Already at the edge of the city of Plymouth, from afar we could see the ships riding at anchor. We found the office of a Norwegian shipping company and asked for work. The official sent us to a small cargo boat named *Sigrid*. It weighed, as I found out later, six thousand register tons. On board we were able to get hired without difficulty; however, our destination was kept from us. This was a precautionary measure commonly taken during the war because it was feared that German submarines would learn the itinerary and sink the ship.

Before we put to sea, the harbor was bombed by German airplanes. Tomaschov and I made it to safety under a bridge together with two young women. As strange at it may seem today, I enjoyed the raid with a kind of grim humor. The spectacle of the red and green defense missiles appeared to me like fireworks even if the harbor was being attacked and ships were being damaged. The raid lasted all night long. I sat on a ledge and one of the girls pressed herself close to me. At that time you didn't know if you would live to see the next day.

Twenty-four hours before we weighed anchor the captain received a sealed envelope with the itinerary and the destination harbor. Only on the high seas was the crew informed of the course. When Glasgow was made known as our destination, I was disappointed.

The *Gullhaug*

In Glasgow we looked for a bigger ship since we assumed that it would cover a greater distance than a smaller one. Finally we found the *Gullhaug*. There were several bullet holes in her bow. The captain had escaped from Norway with the ship when the Germans marched in. We reported on board ship and got hired, Tomaschov as an ordinary seaman and I as a galley hand. The *Gullhaug* was carrying machines. First we had to wait until a convoy was assembled. It was clear from this that a longer trip was planned, since no ship was allowed to put to sea for a longer distance without a protective escort.

In the meantime, Lizzy was already in Chicago. She knew nothing of my intentions. I planned to surprise her with my arrival and imagined how I would suddenly stand in front of her in America.

At Sea

When I heard that the ship was not going to America, but to Canada – namely to Sydney – I was discontented. However, I kept my hopes up with the thought that everything would work out in its own good time. During the trip I asked the captain to be allowed to work as an ordinary seaman like Tomaschov, since the cook was homosexual and was bothering me; moreover, I liked the job of an ordinary seaman better. The convoy, consisting of twenty ships, was accompanied by five small, fast battleships. The *Gullhaug* carried along depth charges for protection against submarines and was equipped with a quadruple anti-aircraft missile. But that was, as the saying goes, "all for nothing." Many ships were sunk by German submarines at that time.

As an ordinary seaman I had to steer the ship. My job was to follow the ship in front of us, making sure that the mast of the *Gullhaug* was in line with its mast. That was more difficult than it sounds. If you lost sight of the mast of the ship in front of you even for an instant, you could get off course because the ship turned away rapidly. For this reason the captain and the helmsman appeared regularly to oversee my work. The captain was – and I don't hesitate to say it – a noble man. His name was Ugland.

Seasick

I got seasick during the trip. I was deathly ill, I wanted nothing else but to lie down in my cabin, but I wasn't allowed to do so. Instead, I had to do my job. I was also talked into eating something. Initially I felt very bad and had to vomit continuously. Slowly my condition got better, and finally I got my sea legs.

A Storm

Part of the crew had been shipwrecked before when a German submarine sank the freighter they had been sailing on. The sailors told me about it as if it had been a trivial affair. But when a terrible storm blew up, even the captain was alarmed. The *Gullhaug* was small and old and had originally been a coastal vessel. The waves towered in front of us like a mountain range. When the ship reached the crest of a wave it tilted downwards almost vertically. The entire ship would tremble and shake before it was slowly picked up again as if by an invisible hand only to tip backwards once more. Sometimes it would lean on its side and be sucked into a vortex. It had barely righted itself when it took off again, only to plunge downwards immediately afterwards in a vertical position. Again and again waves crashed over the ship. The captain stood behind me and read out the compass bearings to me. I could stay on course only with great difficulty because the ship didn't respond to the tiller anymore.

A yellow, cast-iron lamp was hanging from the mast, and in the course of the storm I was ordered to bring it down so it couldn't do any damage if the storm tore it loose. Just when I was about to climb up the mast, the lantern fell down and hit me on the head. The brim of my cap softened the force of its fall a little, but it hit my eye so hard that I lost my balance. A sailor rushed to my aid, but my eye swelled up so much that I couldn't see anything for a while. In the midst of the chaos a certain fatalism gradually set in. I thought to myself: if the ship does make it, fine; if it doesn't make it, that's fine, too. The storm lasted an entire afternoon and all through the night. Only on the next morning did the violent storm finally abate. The ocean was as smooth as glass. We saw that the convoy had disappeared. We also had lost all contact with it since our radio had been broken. In the captain's opinion, our situation was not necessarily disadvantageous. The submarines were usually on the lookout for convoys and attacked them, so as a single ship we were less conspicuous. On the other hand, we were without protection. Moreover, we had to travel more slowly, since the motors had been damaged by the storm. Normally it took eight days to go from England to Canada — we were at sea for fourteen days. Later I learned that the effectiveness of the convoy's protective escort was questionable anyway. If a ship were hit, the convoy would first move on to reach safety. Only on the next day would the search for survivors begin.

The Fight

Whenever Tomaschov and I were together, we spoke only German since we felt most comfortable speaking it. That displeased the two Lapps on board. From the beginning, they imagined that we were spies. When one of them was very drunk, he cursed at us and started to harass us. We tried to avoid him, but we couldn't shake him. Suddenly he pulled a knife on Tomaschov. A Norwegian immediately threw himself between the two, and the Lapp was locked up until he was sober. We avoided him from then on. The captain was on our side. That was the main thing.

To Canada

The rest of our journey proceeded smoothly and without a convoy. On the way we had to scrape the deck with a scraper. Later we were handed cans of paint and told to paint the railing. The last stretch was beautiful, the night was starlit. It was then that I fell in love with seafaring . . . When seagulls appeared, I knew we were near land. "American seagulls," I thought and felt very happy.

It kept getting colder and colder. At that point we weren't very far from Newfoundland. We first reached Pugwash and went on land there. It was covered with snow and ice, so it felt like Greenland to me. We stopped only briefly, loaded wood, and set sail for Sydney.

In the Harbor of Sydney

Sydney is a busy, middle-sized harbor. People of different races discharged our cargo. During the day we had to paint the exterior of the ship. I was suspended from the bow on a board held by ropes and had time to think, but I couldn't come up with a plan for getting from Sydney to America. So I decided to return to England on the *Gullhaug* and make a new attempt from there. Independently of me, Tomaschov reached the same decision. To be sure, I did try to make contact with Canadian Jews, but my efforts were in vain. Anyway, I wouldn't have been permitted to leave the ship since you were always hired for a round trip. We rode at anchor in Sydney for three weeks. When we set out for England, we were accompanied by another convoy. I never saw the two Lapps again.

London

After ten days we put in at Greenrock, the port of Glasgow where our ship was unloaded. The crew was given a week off, and Tomaschov and I were determined to try it anew on the *Gullhaug*. After all, we trusted the captain, who was like a father to us. We spent our time off in London. Posters with "The enemy is listening" painted on them could be found all over the city and in Glasgow. The English army had not yet begun to fight but numerous merchant ships had already been sunk. That was possibly the reason for the popularity of the English seamen. We had ourselves a good time. We had money, and the future was far, far away.

The Next Crossing

Our next destination, we found out at sea, was the port of Halifax in Canada. Once again, I was disappointed. Since I couldn't resign myself to trying it for a third time, I considered leaving the ship at the next best opportunity without officially resigning. This is called "jumping ship." To leave the ship without permission is considered an offense that is punishable even in times of peace. During the war, abandoning ship was even more severely punished, because of the fear of espionage. I was in a quandary about leaving the ship secretly: I enjoyed seafaring, and besides that, I was unaware of the danger a sailor is exposed to during war. I also had a bad conscience at the thought of disappointing the captain. All in all, seafaring had been good to me. I was taken in by a community, saw something of the world, earned money, and didn't spend anything during the journey. So I weighed both sides and in the end decided to try it a third time, which meant leaving the ship only when we reached the United States. However, at the port in Halifax Tomaschov suddenly took the lead.

Jumping Ship

I was still busy on board when Tomaschov went into the city and established contacts. He had told a businessman, a Russian Jew, that two Jewish refugees from Austria were on the way to their relatives in America. The very same afternoon we went ashore without permission and spent the night with the Jewish family. That was "jumping ship." I never saw the captain again. For a long time I felt guilty when I thought about him. But by the same token, I couldn't help but think of Lizzy. Tomaschov, on the other hand, only lived for the present. He did everything out of a love of adventure.

On to Montreal

The next morning we went to Montreal by train. We barely had any money – normally you get paid when you complete your stint. The Jewish businessman who knew our circumstances paid for our ticket and got us new clothes, since we didn't want to be immediately recognized as sailors with our leather jackets, caps, and boots. It was bitterly cold in Montreal. I was frozen stiff and there were mountainous snow piles along roadsides everywhere. For the first time I saw the skyscrapers everyone had been marveling about in Europe. We looked up the address we had been given and were able to hide out for two months with the relatives of the Jewish businessman from Halifax.

Windsor

First we were preoccupied, thinking how we could get into the United States. Finally we found out that there was a city in the north – Windsor – where one part was located in Canada and the other in America. Officially we weren't allowed to enter the United States since we didn't have a visa.

Mountain Police[1]

At that time, the Canadian government had passed a law which was supposed to prevent the immigration of Jews. I had started looking for illegal employment since I needed money to carry out my plan. One day, when I came home from my job search, two men from the Canadian Mountain police[2] were waiting in the kitchen for me. Tomaschov had already been arrested. We were taken to the police station and interrogated. The policemen were very friendly when they heard our story. They even consoled us. But in the end they sent us off on a train to Halifax, because the captain had submitted a report in which he had registered us as missing. It was the beginning of March. We were locked up at the harbor in a prison meant mainly for sailors like us who had jumped ship. Nearly all nationalities were represented, but especially Greeks, Chinese, and Dutch. We became friends with some of them.

In Prison

Food in prison was good. For the first time in my life, I ate corn, which at home was only used in dog food and as pig feed. It tasted great. I really liked prison at first. Nobody was charged with anything. In addition, women from the Jewish community visited us regularly and bought us everything we needed. It had gotten around that we were refugees, thanks to the captain of the *Gullhaug* who reported that we were refugees from Hitler, so we weren't suspected of being spies. We – Tomaschov and I – asked the women, who for the most part were married to influential men,

---

[1] This is the heading in the German original. The author must mean Mounted Police.

[2] Taken from the German original.

to help us immigrate legally to the United States. However, there were Canadian laws which made that impossible, among other things because we had left the ship illegally. They advised us to return to England and wait for the quota, as was required in order to emigrate.

Pegasus

The group of people in the common room at our prison changed constantly, because everyday captains with lists appeared looking for trimmers, galley hands, or sailors for a crossing to Europe. You were free to go if you got hired to serve on a ship. When Tomaschov and I had to admit our plans had failed, we signed up on a Greek ship, the *Pegasus*. I chose it because I liked the name. It was bigger than the *Gullhaug* and was carrying wheat. The difference between the Norwegian and the Greek ship was like day and night. The Norwegians were unionized, friendly, spoke English and German, and the division of labor was perfectly clear. The Greeks, on the other hand, were unfriendly and xenophobic. The work we had to do changed every day. In addition, the captain was surly. A floating village would have been a more suitable name for the ship. Goats and chickens, the latter in a covered hut on deck, were kept for food supplies. Tomaschov called the ship Noah's Ark. When we docked at Swansea, I was disillusioned. I definitely decided to give up any attempts to get to America by ship and to try instead the legal path. At the end of the trip the captain refused to pay me. He forked over a couple pounds only after I applied some pressure. It wasn't close to the amount that was due me. We went to the Seamen's Union, which later got us the money. The English border guards, however, didn't want to let us leave the ship. Because the war had broken out, our permits to stay were automatically extended, but the officials explained to us that we had left Great Britain of our own free will and that on board the *Gullhaug* we had been on Norwegian soil and now on the *Pegasus* we were on Greek soil. For this reason we had forfeited the right to be considered refugees. They took our passports and disappeared. The thought of having to go back to Canada on the

Greek ship made me feel desperate. Because the ship wasn't guarded, we were able to go ashore the very same day, and we traveled to London by train.

Saying Farewell to Tomaschov

First we looked up the Czech Consulate and then the Jewish Committee. They promised us that if we enlisted in the Czech Legion they would straighten things out with the police. They would make sure we got a permit to stay. After that we put up at a refugee hostel in Paddington. The next morning Tomaschov told me, to my surprise, that he would return to Swansea and go on board the *Pegasus* again. He explained that he decided he couldn't join the legion.

Encounter in Swansea

I accompanied Tomaschov as far as the harbor and said good-bye to him thinking that I would never see him again. I didn't want to wait for the ship to leave. But I ended up staying in Swansea for another month because I met a girl. Her father was black and a ship's cook from Jamaica; her mother came from Cardiff. I was strongly attracted to the girl. We stayed together the entire time until I had to go back to London because my money had run out.

London 1941

In London I was supported by the Czech Refugee Trust Fund. The organization's wealth came from the Czech gold reserves, which had been saved from Hitler's grasp in a risky mission carried out during the Nazi invasion. I returned to Paddington, where I lived in a hostel managed by the Czech Trust, located right next to the Austrian Center. There was little food and I was hungry like so many others at that time . . . The hostel was managed by Sudeten German refugees. Once I was awakened from my sleep by an explosion, but I paid no attention to it. Instead, I turned over and fell back to sleep. When I woke up, half of the hostel had been destroyed by a bomb. From my window I could see only rubble.

Eva

At the Austrian Center, as the name indicates, Austrian refugees met. Among them numbered many Jews. They were, for the most part, not politically minded. They went to the center because they were foreigners in London and could meet their fellow countrymen there. It was in the basement. Some rooms had been fixed up as a little café. The atmosphere was friendly, sometimes even gay. It was at the café that I met the sister of an Austrian pianist. At that time Eva was working as a temporary waitress there. She was extraordinarily pretty. Her sister had remained in Vienna with her parents. Her father was a Catholic, her mother a baptized Jew. Eva was very Viennese. She had been educated at the Sacré-Coeur. Together with an aunt she had escaped from Austria after the Anschluss in 1938: the aunt had found a position as a cook, and Eva was able to leave with a transport that had been organized by the Quakers. (At that time the Dutch organization *Gildemaster* was especially concerned with the fate of half-Jews and did what it could for them). I fell in love with Eva and she with me. When I met her, she lived at a privately owned house, in a bed-sitting-room.

Life in London

Half a year later we got married. Eva had a room of her own. The toilet was in the hallway as was the bathroom, which could be used once a week. A hundred thousand English people live like this – many of them until they die. Housing conditions of this kind have always existed in London. Nonetheless, it's an expensive affair. Since there are no cooking facilities, you always have to eat out. Tea is about all you can cook on one gas burner, and for that you even have to put in a coin first. Of course you don't have your own furniture. If you want to feel at home, it's very important that you get on well with the landlady. She is often a widow who has invested her life savings in a boardinghouse. She tidies up and makes sure that order prevails. You are constantly under scrutiny. The atmosphere is cold for the most part. The majority of the tenants are single.

The Wedding

After we got married, Eva and I moved into a boardinghouse close by. We got married in a civil ceremony. Another young couple whom we knew from the Austrian Center were our witnesses. We didn't invite anybody to the wedding. Afterwards we went to a snack bar where we met Eva's aunt. She invited us for coffee and cake. The aunt was an old maid, inherently anti-male, and of course against the wedding. What we saw as a reason to get married, she considered an argument against it: we owned nothing and there was no future. Although the aunt was a Jewess, to be sure (she never was baptized), she was nonetheless anti-Jewish. That was, I assume, also a reason why she didn't like me.

Lizzy

I didn't have a bad conscience when I thought about Lizzy. I had tried everything without accomplishing anything. Finally I had given up any hope of ever being with her again. "That's the end of it," I thought. If we had gotten married before she emigrated to America, then I would have had something in hand worth waiting for. But as it was, I was empty-handed.

Mail from Vienna

Around that time I received mail from my grandmother in Vienna. (My father had already escaped to Slovakia with my mother and sister, and I got news from them only now and then.) My grandmother wrote that she was prohibited from shopping except at certain times. In addition, as a Jewess her rations were significantly smaller than those of the rest of the population and she had to wear the yellow star. Later on I heard that my grandmother physically shrank during that time. She supposedly became very tiny. Uncle Elias and his wife, too, had to wear the Star of David – as a result they didn't leave their apartment anymore. Anyone who lived in Vienna must have realized that Jews were being persecuted there. Jews weren't allowed to use the streetcar, couldn't sit down on park benches anymore, and were completely humiliated. Suddenly they were gone. Was there any possible explanation other than that they had been deported? Even the newspapers had reported that they had been taken to the East in order to work there. Many Viennese Jews had friends and acquaintances from the time before the Anschluss who couldn't have failed to realize what had happened and what was still happening.

Relatives

Meanwhile my father was trying to get my grandmother into Slovakia, but he didn't succeed. A couple of times he sent her money and packages with sausage, bacon, and cheese. In Slovakia there was still plenty of everything. At this point it was already a clerical-fascist state headed by a priest, Father Tiso. The radio stirred up hatred against Jews. Many were baptized at that time in the hope of being able to survive . . . my parents, too. However, baptism only protected them up until 1944, when the Germans marched in and started to deport the Jews following a partisans' revolt.

Emma

Emma, my grandmother's former maid, had become her only

help in Vienna. She brought her food and did her shopping. (If someone had reported her during the war for helping Jews and supplying them with eggs and butter, she would no doubt have gotten into a lot of trouble.)

The Political Situation

When I heard on the radio that Hitler had attacked Russia, I was happy, since he now had to reckon with a new enemy. As was known, Stalin was bound to Germany by a non-aggression pact. As soon as the Communists themselves experienced the Nazis, their attitude changed abruptly. By that time I had already written off the continent. I wasn't even despondent after the defeat of France. When Dunkirk fell, a Czech regiment that had been involved in the fighting escaped to England. Many professional soldiers and officers from the old Czech army were numbered among them. They now began to organize the Czechoslovakian Armed Brigade. The Czech exile government in London was recognized by the English, and the English people never gave us the feeling that we were a burden. They considered us allies.

Drafted into the Exile Army

In 1942 I was finally drafted into the artillery of the Czech exile army. I received a train ticket and the assurance that Eva would be able to join me as soon as I had completed basic training. Thus it wasn't hard for me to say good-bye. I was also relieved that my financial problems were resolved for the time being. The barracks consisted only of a number of wooden huts and they were located near Shakespeare's birthplace, in Leamington Spa. The day of my arrival I was given a uniform and received a rifle. Drills began first thing the next morning.

Anti-Semitism in the Exile Army

I was soon forced to realize that I had gotten myself into a hell of a mess. I only spoke a few words of Czech and therefore was treated as a Jew and a German. There were hardly any Jews in the exile army and even fewer who only spoke German. We were harassed all day long and had to do the most disgusting work. We had to clean the latrines, we were yelled at when we made the beds, and we were ordered to peel the potatoes. The German-speaking Jews were known as "bloody Germans." But it was clear to everyone that the Jews were the only ones who spoke German in the Czech exile army. Nobody dared to be overtly anti-Jewish, so the German language was used as a pretext for expressing anti-Semitic sentiments. It was a vicious circle: we didn't speak Czech and because we didn't speak Czech we were yelled at. There were even Czech nationalists among the noncommissioned and commissioned officers who were Fascists. The officers restrained themselves because they were concerned with their careers. We felt very uneasy at the thought of being sent to the front together with the other soldiers. We had to consider in all seriousness that they might kill us.

However, I slowly learned Czech, and what's more, Czech Communists and Jews joined the exile army after the beginning of Hitler's Russian campaign. The Jews came from Palestine. For the most part they weren't Communists. They were originally from Czechoslovakia and very consciously stood up for their Jewishness. There were so many of them that they made up a third of the artillery group. They put the Czechs in their place. So the situation did improve. We could still feel the anti-Semitism, but it didn't bother us so much anymore. Moreover, the Czech Communists showed their solidarity and stood up to our antagonists. And, not least of all, we continuously received new Jewish recruits who were harassed in place of us older ones.

Eva

The head of the post office in Leamington Spa, a certain Robertson, whom I met by chance while apartment-hunting, offered me an attic apartment, because he sympathized with my being a soldier in the exile army. Eva moved in there. After that my superiors harassed me even more often. For instance, I was denied leave under the pretext that my rifle wasn't properly cleaned. In any case, you were only allowed to spend the night outside of the barracks if you were on furlough or had the weekend off, and for this reason their harassment affected me all the more.

Daily Life

The head of the post office was not the only one who was helpful. I remember the English people in general as friendly and accommodating. Until Eva arrived, I had a widow do the laundry I accumulated as a soldier. I almost always found a bar of chocolate or a pack of cigarettes in the ironed clothes that I picked up.

England

In April England is its most beautiful. That's when the crocuses are in bloom. The English give you a lift anywhere, even if it's out of their way. At that time I was already able to communicate quite well in English. In Leamington Spa there was a soldiers' canteen run by local society ladies. Coffee, tea, and cookies were served . . . You could also order a warm meal – beans and toast.

Ruth

In the summer of 1942 Eva's and my daughter Ruth was born in Leamington Spa. I visited Eva in the hospital and brought her some fuchsia. Very happy with my personal life, I was hardly affected by the war. But whenever I thought about my relatives on the continent, I was depressed. Although I tried to bring my sister to England, I didn't succeed.

Walton on the Naze

We were moved from Leamington Spa to the coast. There were about three or four thousand of us. The place on the coast was called Walton on the Naze. We exercised every morning on the beach. The area had been evacuated out of fear of a German invasion. Eva followed soon with our child. I liked the landscape extremely well: flat meadows, lighthouses, bays with old boats right at the water's edge. The ocean on England's coast is cold everywhere. In every village there is one of those beautiful

Anglican churches, as well as Methodist, Baptist, and Quaker churches. You could also find a Roman Catholic church.

Identity

At that time I would have preferred not being Jewish. Although I didn't plan to renounce Judaism, I suffered from the anti-Semitism. I didn't know anymore who I was. Was I Austrian? Czech? Was I Jewish? Or already English? I had to be something, anything, I told myself.

Transfers

In Walton on the Naze we were a part of the coast guard. Our cannons were set up along the ocean. We practiced using them mornings as well as afternoons.

A couple months later I was transferred to Huntington, which is located near Cambridge . . . From there I was sent to Beccles in Suffolk. We only stayed in Beccles a few months . . . All of England is pretty with its lawns and hedges . . . My wife and child lived across from the barracks in the house of a colonel in the Salvation Army. The entire family was musical.

One time I was confined to quarters because I had spoken to my wife, who had passed by during my guard duty. My wife bought me a pipe for the days that I was locked up. After that I no longer smoked cigarettes . . .

From Beccles we moved on to Chart in Somerset. It's nestled in a hilly landscape. I didn't like it there very much. We lived in tents in the forest. The Americans were already in Chart. I noticed the segregation of the blacks from the whites. The military police saw a lot of action thanks to the many pubs. The blacks formed their own group . . . I remember that they were thrown out of some of the inns. At this time my wife and child were living on the coast, in Lyme Regis. Next we were transferred to Scotland, to Kelso on the river Tweed. The area was romantically wild. We didn't stay there very long but moved on to Edinburgh for maneuvers. Edinburgh impressed me as a city . . . You can see the northern lights. . . a pink light . . . It's beautiful . . . That was the first time I had been to Edinburgh.

In the meantime my wife moved with our child to Oxford to stay with an acquaintance from the Czech army and his wife who had rented a house. Whenever it was possible, I spent a few days of vacation there. Last of all I was in Bridlington in Yorkshire. The houses were all empty. Now and then you could see a couple old people and a stray dog. We were living in a ghost town.

Thoughts from Back Then

At that time America had already entered the war, and I knew that the Allies would win the war even if it were to last a bit longer. Above all I thought that all problems would be solved once the war was won. But I didn't receive letters from my parents anymore. At that point I hadn't heard anything about the "systematic" extermination of Jews. It is true I knew that there were ghettos and concentration camps, but it never entered my head what was really behind it all.

Invasion

After D-day the soldiers felt certain that they would soon be transferred to the continent. The Czech anti-Semites in the army had been forced on the defensive, especially by the Communists, who were well organized and expected to be influential in the future. We received a few days' furlough, and I went to Oxford to be with my family until we had to embark. The entire Czech exile army along with their cannons had to take position in a meadow in Essex and had to march to the harbor. The streets were filled with English, American, and Polish soldiers. We boarded a huge ship that took us to Avromange in Normandy, in the *département* of Calvados.

In Normandy

I was in France for the first time. Avromange had been completely leveled, so was Caen. The German army had retreated but they were trying to hold on to Dunkirk. At that time only women were still living in the bombed out houses. Cars and bombed-out tanks burned in the streets. Soldiers killed in action lay on the ground. It was the first battlefield I had ever seen and it was a shock. We saw action outside of Dunkirk; however, we had no direct contact with the enemy. We shot into Dunkirk and the Germans there shot back at us. Later I found out that a cousin of mine who had been in the Czech exile army had been killed at Dunkirk; however, I had never met him.

Living in tents was hard in the winter. Our four cannons were

lined up in front of the tents. We shelled the town all day long —·
that kept us busy most of the time.

Once I had a two-day furlough in St. Omer, a very old town
that hadn't been destroyed.

Despite the war I found France to be beautiful. I resolved to
return again during peacetime. I was also given a week's furlough
to go to Oxford, and later on I had a few days to go to Lille on the
Belgian border.

An Encounter

On my first evening in Lille I met a young woman. It turned
out that she was a prostitute. She took me to her room and I stayed
the night. She wasn't pretty, but very nice. The next morning she
wouldn't even accept money from me. On the contrary, she gave
me American cigarettes.

War

During my furlough, fighting on the front intensified. When I
returned to my unit, they were wiping the blood and brains of one
of my tent mates off our cannon. My thinking had already conformed
to the general emotional state, and I was only glad that it wasn't me.

Men and Women

At the first opportunity I had I went back to Lille to look for
the girl, but her apartment was locked up. I knocked until the hair-
dresser whose shop was below her apartment appeared and told me
that she and her girlfriend had been carted off by the police. Later
I found out that she had gotten involved with a German soldier.
Allegedly she was crazy about men in uniform. I went to Oxford
on furlough again, to a world without problems, so I told myself.
In France everything had been destroyed by the war, even the
relationship between the sexes. The men had gone to war or were
called up to do national work service and the women stayed home
alone. The soldiers who passed through gave the women canned
goods, and the women slept with them in return.

In Germany

In 1945, the last year of the war, we were transferred to Germany. It was a strange feeling to return. It was after all something like "home" for me . . . especially the German language . . . In Germany we weren't involved in any fighting anymore. Our main responsibility was guarding refugee and prison camps. I felt sorry for the prisoners, but had no contact with them.

The End of the War

I found out about the end of the war on a narrow path in France. I wanted to be alone to gather my thoughts.

On to Czechoslovakia with the Army

At the end of the war the Czech exile army was separated from the British army and joined up with the Americans. We were supposed to back them up in the battle for Czechoslovakia. Most of us wanted to participate in the liberation of Prague anyway. During the trip through Germany we saw the extent of the destruction. At that point I didn't yet know what had happened to my parents. But in the meantime the British had liberated the concentration camp Bergen-Belsen, and I suspected the dimension of the catastrophe that had descended on Germany. So I considered the mass destruction a Biblical punishment. The buildings in ruins, the collapsed bridges . . . I was convinced that it had been necessary. "That's the war!" I said to myself. I saw the destruction in Coblenz, Mainz, and Darmstadt . . . Würzburg and Fürth had been completely destroyed. Only when I saw Nuremberg bombed out did I feel a sense of regret since I had a romantic image of this town. Finally we reached the Bohemian Forest, where we were billeted in Kolinetz.

Refugees

The villages were decorated in our honor and banners welcomed the Czech army. Everywhere people ran into the streets to cheer us. At that time Czechoslovakia was not yet Communist.

En route we met streams of German-speaking refugees from the East, I believe from Transylvania. The people were fleeing from the Russians on wooden handcarts, and they herded their livestock in front of them. The sight of them pulled at my heartstrings. The Czechs treated them badly, even refusing to let the animals have any water. It was a depressing sight. Many refugees were hungry. We had a bucket with leftovers and when I wanted to pass it around, a Czech officer knocked it out of my hand. Nonetheless, I distributed cigarettes and chocolate. There was, however, a strict prohibition against fraternization. In the meantime the citizens of Prague revolted against the Germans, but we had to wait in the Bohemian Forest, since there was an agreement that the Russians would liberate Prague.

In the Bohemian Forest

Initially we had the order to look for *werewolves* in the Bohemian Forest, that is, "to play soldier." I never got to see one. But by the same token we had the opportunity to observe what went on in the villages. All of the possessions of the Sudeten Germans were taken away from them "legally": radios, bikes, cars. They had to wear white armbands and had to observe a curfew. I was in Klatovy (Klatau), Sucice (Schüttenhofen) and Kasperske Hory (Bergreichenstein). The Sudeten Germans left the entire area, and the Czechs arrived slowly. I got along better with the Sudeten Germans than with the Czechs because of our common language if nothing else. In Kolinetz I met the relatives of the owner of a castle . . . The former owner had been killed by Czech civilians before we had marched in. Part of the family had fled, and the rest, mainly women, had been locked up in the working quarters. During the day they had to work on the estate. In the past the Czechs had to work the fields for the German masters as day laborers; now the former masters had to slave away for their former day laborers. Many years later I met the son of the former owner in Vienna and told him what I had seen. I only regretted that the war had such consequences.

One time a Czech woman approached me and complained that the Jews had returned again. She wanted to curry favor with me because she didn't know that I was Jewish. "What a beautiful homeland this is," I told her before I left her standing there.

Searching for My Family

I didn't want to remain in Czechoslovakia, I wanted to return to Oxford to be with my wife and child. However, before I left, I wanted to know what had happened to my family. I mailed a letter to Miklos, the place where I had gotten the last letter from my parents, and I received a message from my sister that she and my mother had been liberated from Theresienstadt by the Russians and were now staying in Miklos. She didn't write anything about my father. I took a furlough from the army, stuffed my backpack with cans, cigarettes, and chocolate, and set off. There weren't any train or bus connections anymore. I went by truck for a while, then by freight train, and the last bit I did on foot. I was traveling at my own risk. Since I was traveling from the American occupied zone into the Russian occupied zone, it was quite possible that I would fall into Russian hands and be suspected of being a spy. Moreover, I didn't understand their language. So whenever I saw a Russian soldier I immediately took cover. The farther I went into Slovakia, the wilder the landscape looked. I was en route for twelve days. The last piece in the High Tatras I traveled by ox cart. The farmer was transporting sacks of grain. I tried to speak Czech to him, but Czechs and Slovaks don't like each other. We went along the Waag River. A thunderstorm blew up, it started to rain. Now and then I got on the cart, or I would walk alongside of it like the farmer. In Miklos I asked my way to the Jewish community. When I found it, they were in the middle of distributing food to the Jews who had returned from the camps. My sister and I saw each other at the same instant. She was overcome by emotion, but I was embarrassed to display my feelings. On our way to mother I found out that my father had been shot during the transport from Oranienburg to Sachsenhausen. Later my sister's husband, who had been in Sachsenhausen with my father for the entire time, told me more details. I didn't feel vengeful – only powerless.

My family was living in a primitive barrack. My mother hadn't expected me. It was an emotional reunion.

The Fate of My Family

In 1941 my parents and my sister had moved from Vienna to Slovakia. Initially they had to struggle against great adversity until my father got a job as a sales representative for a leather factory and traveled professionally in Slovakia and Hungary. However, they were unable to find an apartment and had to sublet. Because of his long absence my father was treated like a stranger in the town where he had been born. The restrictions had become increasingly drastic; however, they hoped that it wouldn't go to extremes. From 1942 on all Jews were taken to labor camps guarded by the Slovakian Hlinka Guard. (The Hlinka movement, to which the Slovakian president Tiso also belonged, was named after a deceased priest. They were more right wing than the conservatives.) The camp was located in Zilina. After the partisans' putsch against Tiso had been put down, the Germans marched into Slovakia and saw to it that the Slovakian government carried out the Nuremberg racial laws. Uncle Heinrich, the worker and Social Democrat with whom I had lived during my stay in Slovakia, was deported to Poland together with his family. I never heard from them again. The same happened to my father's sister, her husband and their two daughters who had the shoe store under the colonnade. Their traces disappear in a Polish camp.

Escape

In the camp my father met a schoolmate who belonged to the Hlinka Guard. In order to save them from deportation, this schoolmate let him, my mother, and sister escape. First they tried to reach the mountains in the East. En route they had considered giving up until they met a Protestant minister who helped them get lodging with a family in the village and supplied them with forged "Aryan" papers. In order not to attract attention, they went to mass regularly. Later my father also sang in the church choir. He feared for his daughter's safety and prayed to God to save her. Then someone who knew him from before reported him to the Germans. But before they could arrest him and his family, some Communists helped them escape to the High Tatras. It was winter. Crossing through a rough area on barely negotiable paths, they reached a logger's cabin. My father had left the gold watch and the little jewelry he had on him with the pastor (he returned everything to me after the war). For three months my parents and my sister hid. The Communists, three young men from the village, supplied them with food in the primitive cabin. One of them fell in love with my sister and stayed with her. When spring came, the Germans began to comb the area. My father, who had diabetes and who was emotionally exhausted, thought it would be better to leave their hiding place and return to the village, but when they showed up they were arrested and taken to the forced labor camp Sered on the Hungarian border.

Sered

A Viennese man by the name of Brunner ran the camp at Sered. The camp inmates were whipped and had to stand outside naked . . . The top capo of the camp police, himself a Jew, was a friend of Brunner and had hidden Brunner for some time when he had been an "illegal" party member. It was part of the Nazis' method to have the Jews themselves compile the list with the names of the prisoners who were to be deported to Poland to the extermination camps. The top capo only received instructions to ready a certain number for transportation, and it was up to him to make the selection. This way he had a certain amount of power. He was from the twentieth district in Vienna, by the way. He propositioned my mother a short time after her arrival, and offered to protect her family if she became his mistress. My mother was forty-two years old at that time and very pretty. She consulted with my father and he agreed to it because of his love for his daughter. From that point on, however, he didn't want to live any longer.

My Father's Death

When the camp was dissolved in 1944, all male inmates were deported to Poland in cattle-cars. My family was supposed to be taken to Theresienstadt, where there was at least a small chance of survival, since the Russians were already close to the border. It was the last thing the top capo did for them. The train stopped at Mährisch Ostrau. It was said that some of the cars were to go on to Theresienstadt, the others to Sachsenhausen. My mother and sister were in a car that went to Theresienstadt, my father and my sister's boyfriend in one that went to Sachsenhausen. My father was fifty-four years old at that time. The family had to say good-bye at the train station. My father was already slipping mentally, but he still grasped what was going on around him . . . Because of his diabetes he should have been treated with insulin on a daily basis . . . A short time later one of his legs became gangrenous. When he couldn't walk any longer, he was shot by the SS. The story was related to me by the man who later married my sister – he had witnessed everything.

Theresienstadt

Theresienstadt was a ghetto with Jewish self-government. Before the Russians liberated it, typhoid and dysentery broke out, which my mother and sister also contracted. (In the end they passed the dysentery on to me. Even today I still suffer its consequences in the form of digestive problems.) The Jewish capo from Sered had no more pull. My mother had to shovel coal from trains. She avoided him.

In Theresienstadt, too, the compilation of deportation lists was the duty of the Jewish Council. By then it was known for certain that gas chambers existed, so the most important principle was to save the youth, although it was obvious that everyone in the Jewish Council (whether Communist, Orthodox, Austrian, French, Dutch, or Dane) wanted to save their own. One time the Red Cross organized a train that went to Switzerland. However, this undertaking was highly suspect because it was feared that the train would really go to Poland . . . But it actually did go to Switzerland . . . In 1945 the Russians liberated the ghetto. In the end my mother, my sister, and her future husband, who had searched for her after his liberation, reached Miklos on a hay wagon, where I was reunited with them.

Back to the Army
After a week I had to report back to the army. My family didn't
want to stay in Slovakia, where the population had always been
prejudiced against Jews. In the meantime the Czechs had expelled
the Sudeten Germans, resulting in many empty apartments and
houses. Now everything happened the other way around. Czechs
from industrial towns as well as Slovaks poured into *Sudetenland*,
that is, what had been the German-speaking part of Czechoslovakia. *Sudetenland* was the spoils. Riffraff came onto the scene
because they hoped for easy money. They took what the Sudeten
Germans had been forced to leave behind. When I returned, my
sister's husband accompanied me, so that he could look for a new
place for his family to live. I wanted to talk him into going to
Vienna, but the borders were closed. The return trip was difficult
again. We had to walk for long distances. By way of Prague we
reached Pilsen, where my unit was stationed, but my brother-in-
law continued on from Pilsen to Marienbad. There he later found
lodging with a Sudeten German family who knew that they had to
leave the country . . . I could have done something for my brother-
in-law but I found the idea of committing robbery repulsive. For
this reason I remained in Pilsen. From the very beginning my
brother-in-law had a good rapport with the Sudeten German
family, or so I was told. When they emigrated to Germany, he took
over their apartment in exchange for a sum of money.

Tomaschov
One day I ran into Tomaschov in Prague. It was a curious
coincidence. We were both very moved and had lunch at the Hotel
Alcron. The longer we talked, the less we understood each other.
Tomaschov had become a Communist and welcomed the
Communist regime in Czechoslovakia. The very thought made me
uneasy and I disagreed with him. We didn't get into a fight, but I
never saw him again.

In *Pekla*, in "Hell"
Those soldiers from the Czech exile army who wanted to leave

Czechoslovakia and return to England had assembled in Pilsen. There was an arrangement whereby all soldiers should return to where they had come from. However, those who decided to stay were allowed to leave the army. All Jews with whom I had contact wanted to return to England and so did all the Czechs who were married to English women. The barrack where we were staying was called *Pekla*, or "hell." Formerly it had served as a theater or a circus. I don't know why it was called this, but it really did become a hell for me because I had to wait so long for my transfer back to England. Of course I didn't want to stay in Czechoslovakia. I thought "go west, young man" . . . More than anything else I needed to lead a normal life. Moreover, my wife wrote me letters urging me to return to Oxford. Soldiers were transported from *Pekla* to England on a regular basis, but for some unknown reason, my turn didn't come. I was afraid I wouldn't get an exit visa and would have to remain in the barrack. In the meantime I had become friends with German-speaking Jews who also spoke Czech. Two of them went to the British Consulate and to the Czech Ministry of War and applied for exit visas and permission to leave the army. At the same time they presented my petition. But I still had to wait two months in *Pekla,* and I returned to England with the last convoy.

Discharge

At that time I considered England my home. We were taken in trucks from Harwich to a small village near London where we were given an open-ended furlough. We were still waiting for the final demobilization, which came a few weeks later. From then on we were civilians.

Reunion

I had been gone from home for five months. Seeing Eva and our child again was wonderful. I can still remember today how happy I was at the time. Soon thereafter we moved to London where we again found a little apartment in Paddington, near the Austrian Center. The building was a bit run down, but it was empty because its occupants had left on account of the German bombings. We lived there together with other refugees.

Job Search

Soon I realized that it was going to be difficult for me to find work. My last report card was in German, and what's more, the English have a different system of education. So I had to take what I was offered . . . I changed jobs twenty times in fifteen years, but I didn't care. Initially it was simply important to me to be able to stay with my wife and child.

My first job was at a lens cutter's in an industrial suburb of London. The company was called Levers Optical Company. In its workrooms mainly lenses, but also microscopes were produced. In the morning a bell rang and we worked continuously until ten o'clock. At that point we had a ten-minute tea break, then we continued working until the bell rang again. The lunch break lasted thirty minutes. The bell would promptly ring again. At 4 p.m. the bell would ring again for a ten-minute tea break, and then at 6 p.m. it would ring for the last time, when the workday ended. I came home rather tired. After a few months I was transferred to the London headquarters, where I had to cut lenses so they fit into the various frames. The work was monotonous. In addition to that I saw no possibility for advancement. When I looked at the drafting instruments which I had carried with me since my escape, my work seemed even more dreary. I had long since lost my textbook for mechanical engineering by Freytag.

My Marriage

Initially I had a very good marriage, though it's true that we had seen little of each other because I was in the military and was away a lot of the time. Moreover, our financial situation had been better. Now we lived together all the time and had little money. Slowly we became estranged. During our fights Eva even threatened suicide . . . One day she wanted to leave me . . . I corresponded with her father. He wrote me that I would always have a hard time with her. Her sister, a famous pianist, had always been the stronger of the two. Eva's greatest desire was to be an actress . . . She played a small part in the film *The Third Man*. She was also cast in an English television show. But she earned too little and I didn't earn enough, so she also worked as a waitress. As a way to improve our situation, I applied for British citizenship.

A British Citizen

A short time after I applied for citizenship, an officer from Scotland Yard visited me in our shabby apartment. I had just given up my job as a lens cutter and he wanted to know why. To my surprise, he knew everything about me, especially what I had done in England. He even knew that I had joined a Zionist youth group in Vienna. At that point Britain was still fighting with Palestine . . . The officer wanted to know if I were still a Zionist and if I still intended to emigrate to Palestine. I answered that I wanted to stay in England and serve the country as a British citizen.

I was in fact awarded citizenship a short time later. I did, however, have to pay a fee of ten pounds. In this time of need I wrote to my father's former boss and asked him for the money, and to my great joy he sent it to me.

Later the British passport enabled me to visit my family in Czechoslovakia.

However, many years went by before it came to that.

Divorce, 1948

That same summer the English family who had left London because of the German bombings returned, and we had to move out. We soon found another boardinghouse, where we lived until our divorce. We fought more and more often, you see, and after one big argument I left the apartment. Eva lost control easily. She worked as a model at that time and met other men that way. It didn't suit me at all, and I was jealous.

When we finalized the divorce, I signed everything I was asked to.

Alone

In the meantime I worked at various jobs, first at a factory which produced beer caps, then at a company for magician's paraphernalia. The products were sold all over the world: jack-in-the-boxes and board games. Next I was employed at a factory where glass buttons were produced. I changed jobs every few months, but I improved my language skills and had contact with English workers. I learned to appreciate the English even more. They were fair and not nosy, neither ironical nor sarcastic. "You don't hit a drowning man," or so goes an English proverb.

I earned only a little. A third of it went for rent. In addition I paid child support for Ruth whenever possible. Each week I picked up our child and went to the zoo with her. Later on Eva moved to her aunt's. At that time my meals consisted mainly of fish and chips . . . sometimes just chips. In spite of this there were days when I was happy. I was lonely, but I found myself in my loneliness. I would wander through the East End down to the docks or Petticoat Lane where there was a Sunday market. Eventually I stopped visiting our child because it broke my heart every time I had to take her back to her mother.

Finders, Keepers

Soon after my divorce I met a young Jewish women from Bremen. I lived with her for a year, and we got along very well. However, like Lizzy, she emigrated to America, and again I wasn't allowed to accompany her since I didn't receive an immigration permit. I stood at the harbor and watched the ship slowly disappear on the horizon. At that time I hated America, a feeling which lasted for some time.

Dorothy

Some time later, during one of my lonely walks, I met Dorothy Manly, a girl from an English working-class family. She worked in an office, her brother at a garage. Dorothy wasn't an educated woman. But I learned a lot about life from her. Together we visited the Tate and the National Gallery, we took trips to the ocean and often went to the opera. Dorothy especially loved the Italian composers. Actually I was happy again. It was just the constant changing of jobs that was a burden to me.

The Jewish Chronicle

Since my divorce the thought of Israel had always been in the back of my mind. After the Holocaust, I was convinced that the Jews needed their own country where they couldn't be persecuted.

Moreover, I had been a member of the *Shomer,* and what I had learned there still influenced me. I read *The Jewish Chronicle* on a regular basis. One day I found an article that described the possibility of going to Israel to work. If you agreed to work in a kibbutz for a year, the travel costs would be paid for in advance. I discussed it with Dorothy. She immediately agreed. The kibbutz which I finally signed up for was called *Ogen* (Anchor). Viennese and Czech Jews had founded and settled it, among them some I knew from my youth in Vienna.

Israel

After I had agreed to a year of service as described in the newspaper, I went to Israel together with Dorothy in spring of 1952. The trip took us to Dover by train, from Dover to Calais, and from there to Paris. We stayed in a small room in the Rue Lafayette, and we visited the Louvre and the Sacré Coeur. The ship on which we sailed to Israel – the *Negbaah* – was anchored at the port of Marseille.

Moroccan Jews with many children and bundles – colorful, like gypsies traveled on the 'tween decks. They stayed on deck all day long. First we arrived in Naples, but we weren't allowed to leave the ship. The trip continued along the coast of Sicily to Crete and from there to Haifa. On the ship I met a Moroccan Jew from Jerusalem who gave me the creeps.

It was an uplifting moment when we finally approached the harbor. The first thing you saw was the silhouette of Mt. Carmel in the distance. It was very hot. Women from some organization brought tea and sandwiches on board for the immigrants. Two members of the kibbutz were already waiting for us at the harbor in a jeep, in order to take us to *Ogen*. I thought that I would now see the desert, and in fact we drove through a subtropical landscape. *Ogen* is located near Tel Aviv, not far away from the ocean. We arrived at the kibbutz consisting of small houses with porches and yards. Everything was in bloom and fragrant. Earlier this place had been a swamp.

Ogen

The kibbutz made an idyllic first impression on me. In the evening its inhabitants were sitting in front of their houses bent over chessboards or going for walks. Children were playing on the paths. The houses had been freshly painted. I believe it was the Sabbath. Radio music was coming from the windows . . . Everyone welcomed us. In the center there was a small round area with a fountain and the dining-hall, the *Chadar Ochel*. Events and meetings took place there. First we were assigned to a family who introduced us to life in the kibbutz. They showed us the rubber factory where tires and rubber sheets for hospitals were produced as well as where to turn in our laundry. Only older people worked in the factory, the younger ones were assigned to farming. The rubber factory brought money to the kibbutz. I liked life there only at the beginning. I didn't hit it off with any of the Viennese Jews I met. They had all become doctrinaire. During their time off, they worked in their front yards, and they had in general developed a narrow-minded outlook. For this reason I had hardly any contact with them. People change at the kibbutz: you have to subordinate yourself to community life, you weren't supposed to criticize, and you were expected to be completely committed to work. As a consequence the members slowly start to resemble one another. Moreover, I really felt isolated from what was going on. I wanted to get to know the country, its religious movements, and the Arabs; however, we were allowed to go to Jerusalem only once in a while, and the possibilities of talking with the Arab population were limited.

Leaving the Kibbutz

The work schedule was such that I was assigned the night shift, while Dorothy worked the day shift. We had been in the kibbutz about six months when she fell in love with another man and moved out of our cabin. I looked for her everywhere, but nobody would tell me where she was. Nobody wants conflict in a kibbutz, everything is supposed to proceed peacefully. Even when someone ends a relationship it's supposed to happen without any fuss. They were probably afraid of me and feared that I would cause a scene – I was in just such a mood, by the way. Only a week later did someone tell me where Dorothy was hiding in the kibbutz. In the meantime I felt like an idiot. Everyone knew where she was and nobody had told me anything. Dorothy and I had a long talk. When I declared that I wanted to leave the kibbutz, nobody stopped me.

Tel Aviv

I was taken to Tel Aviv, where I found work at the airport with

Bedek, a company that serviced airplanes. They made spare parts and did maintenance and repair work. Along with some Austrian Jews and Jewesses, I worked in the administration of the warehouse. My co-workers were very open and approachable. Nonetheless I felt lonely. Only Haifa fascinated me. You could meet Arab Jews and drink Turkish coffee . . . I met a Catholic priest there. He was thirty years old and his name was Bruno Husar.

Bruno Husar

Bruno Husar was Jewish and Dominican. As a student he was baptized by a Father Menasse who was also Jewish, but had become Catholic and worked as a missionary in Israel. Every day I would walk the forty-five minutes to Father Husar in order to talk with him. He wanted to build a Jewish-Christian church with Hebrew as its language instead of Latin. He also wanted to integrate Jewish traditions into the church. It was all conceived along Jewish-nationalistic lines. In the evening he would climb on the roof of the convent and pray there. Meeting him was enriching. Jesus was a Jew. The Sermon on the Mount had already impressed me very much in my youth. Because of Father Bruno I began to devote my time to the study of Christianity.

Back to England

In the meantime I continued working at the airplane factory until I had saved enough money for my trip back. All in all I stayed in Israel for a total of fifteen months. Leaving was extremely difficult for me. For Israelis, leaving the country is the same as treason. I, however, did intend to return.

In London

In London I found a room in my old boardinghouse. I felt free then and without responsibility, and intended to live like that for some time. As a result, I didn't get in touch with Ruth and Eva.

I had an easier time than before in my job search: my English had gotten very good. By then I thought and dreamed only in

English. One morning I realized that I had even talked to myself in English.

In 1954 I found work with BICC – British Insulated Cable Construction. They installed cables in cities and villages all over the world. I was hired as a design engineer and had to draw plans for the laying of the cables.

Marianne

On one of my weekends off I met Marianne Chavernes, a Huguenot from Paris. She had studied in England and was working for an import-export company. Of all the women I knew, she probably loved me the most. When my company transferred me to Edinburgh, she promised to follow. But Marianne became very ill. She had to be taken to a hospital in London and later needed to be nursed for years. We gradually lost track of one another.

Edinburgh

I liked Edinburgh as much as I had liked it the first time when I was still in the Czech exile army. In London I had been continuously under stress: everything was so far apart and there was so little time. Here life was much easier. I also liked the buildings and streets. All around, mountains rise up, and in fall the landscape is transformed by the magic of the red and yellow colors.

Hilde, 1956

Because of my job with the cable company I traveled all over Scotland – to mountain villages and isolated farms, but also to towns like Dundee, Glasgow, Aberdeen, Inverness, and Perth. I even got to know the islands. In the house where I lived, I met Hilde, a young German woman from Swabia. She worked for *Caritas* (a Catholic relief organization), had studied in Freiburg, and had become a social worker. Her job was to care for the German prisoners of war who had remained in Scotland and for the au-pair girls who worked here. A German priest lived in Bradford who only seldom came to Edinburgh – Hilde acted as a contact person when he wasn't there.

At Christmas I helped her put up a Christmas tree. She invited me that evening – it was the first time that I had taken part in a Christmas celebration. Hilde's engagement had just been broken off. We were both lonely and quickly became close.

Marriage

We got married half a year later. Hilde quit her job because a child was already on the way. We rented a small house on the ocean. In my time off I took care of the yard. Up to then I had only lived in bed-sitting-rooms.

My wife was clear-headed and very well educated. Her father had been a National Socialist, even a member of the SA, as I found out from her. However, I was able to convince myself that he wasn't a racist.

Hannah and Wendy

Hannah was born in 1958.

I led a new kind of life. Hilde was very easygoing. I always looked forward to coming home.

In Edinburgh we had another daughter, Wendy.

We had many Scottish acquaintances and also German ones. On Sunday we took trips to Crammond, which is on the ocean. You could row out on the water in boats or simply lie down in the grass at the edge of the forest or take walks on the heath. I had become a member of the Labor party in the meantime. I also supported their cause at election time.

Vienna, 1959

I returned to Austria for the first time in twenty years to meet my mother in Vienna. My sister hadn't received an exit visa. We stayed at the Hotel Post on Fleischmarkt. After my arrival I went to Leopoldstadt. Much still lay in ruins, although there were some new buildings. The places evoked pleasant feelings in me, less so the people I encountered. Despite the familiarity of the streets and buildings, Vienna had become a foreign city for me. It's true that everything was still there – the parks, Karmelitermarkt, the Danube Canal,but I didn't come across anyone from my childhood and youth. I wouldn't have gone to Vienna of my own accord, but my mother was so attached to the city and had talked me into meeting her there and into considering returning. I found some stores which still looked the same, like the bookstore *Abheiter* on Taborstraße, where as a high school student I used to exchange my school books between grades.

It was good to hear German again. I didn't equate it with National Socialism. Not for a moment did I consider punishing an entire people for the crimes of one member. On the contrary, I was convinced that under certain conditions the same thing could have happened in other countries. What I felt most intensely was grief. At times when I walked in the street looking at buildings it occurred to me that perhaps old Nazis were living there.

Like so many things, my uncle Elias' stationer's store was gone. In its place I found a plumber's shop.

My mood vacillated. In Quay Park the trees were blooming. I went to the fountain; everything was in its old place, unchanged, and still it was as if it had been locked away in some vault for many years.

I didn't speak to a single soul. They appeared strangely obstinate to me. After having lived in England I was used to people smiling at each other when they got onto a bus. Here they sat in the streetcars stone-faced. They looked fierce and harried. I thought, "There must be a reason for it." They certainly had lived through a lot: bombs, foreign soldiers, the death of relatives. The people took no notice of each other. The Prater that I visited had changed completely. In my memory I associated it with people, music, the merry-go-round – I had gone there often with my family. Now it looked desolate. There were only booths that weren't even open. Almost nothing was open. I walked up and down the main avenue one time. As a child I had always collected the horse chestnuts that had fallen from the trees. The Café Constantin where I drank a *Kracherl* (a soft drink) as a first grader was still open.

The next day I looked around Leopoldsgasse where I had gone to Talmud Torah. I found only a vacant lot . . . The synagogue had burned down during *Kristallnacht*. I thought about the many Jews who had lived in Leopoldstadt. "That's all over," I said to myself without wishing for revenge. Then I moved on to *Schüttel* where Lizzy had lived. It looked just the same. That too moved me more than I had expected. It forced me to imagine what my life with Lizzy would have been like. I started to feel melancholy . . . Only the knowledge that I had a wife and children in England consoled me.

In the evening my mother told me about her family and how things were in Czechoslovakia. She wanted me to return to Vienna. I replied that I found Vienna repulsive. Of course you didn't see any swastikas, but I didn't want to have anything to do with former Nazis and their sympathizers anymore. In general I didn't want to be reminded of the problems. Everywhere there was only one topic of discussion: "The Russians . . . the Russians!" and "the rapes." It was at times like this that I always wanted to ask: And what did the Nazis do to the Russians? And what about us Jews?

Making Plans Again

Strangely enough, after having been in Vienna I found myself thinking about the city more often than before. Above all it was clear to me that I wasn't a "true" Englishman. You can only be English if you have a grandfather buried in an English cemetery.

It's even more difficult to become a Scot. Scottish life revolves around clans. You always remain a foreigner. This perception was, of course, *my* problem, which I told myself that I had brought on myself. My acquaintances were always nice to me, they were happy that Hilde and I had settled in so well. They probably wouldn't have understood my thoughts at all.

Pittermann

One day I read in the paper that Bruno Pittermann, the candidate of the Socialist party, had become vice-chancellor of Austria. I immediately remembered that he had been my teacher of German, history, and geography at the Arsenal for two years. After some hesitation I wrote him a letter in which I hinted what my fate had been. To my surprise he responded with an invitation. He asked me why I didn't return to Austria. If I should decide to do so after all, he would assist me. Naturally, that was very tempting, since I thought about Vienna more and more.

To Germany

In the meantime a friend of my wife had visited us and talked Hilde into moving to Germany. The entire country, she said, was being reconstructed, and the economic situation was better than anywhere else. In addition she'd have her relatives in Eschenbach when we first got there. My wife pressed for a decision, and I agreed to go. Nonetheless, I left Edinburgh with a heavy heart.

Eschenbach

Eschenbach is a small German town. The inhabitants were exactly what you would expect of a small German town . . . They didn't know anything about anything. Everything was very clean, very orderly. The motto was: Everything for the home. Thriftiness. Hard work. On Sunday you went out for coffee and cake – miserable.

My Father-in-Law

Hilde's father was a very versatile man. He was different from the rest of the Eschenbachers. When he returned from Russia, he had been very burdened by what he had experienced. Even during the Nazi period he had voiced the opinion that the war couldn't be won on moral grounds. The atrocities that the German army had committed wouldn't allow it. Ever since then he was very reserved, and he remained so until he died.

Munich, Brown-Boveri

Soon we moved to Munich, where I started to work for Brown-Boveri as a technical translator. Nobody said a word during the entire work day. The supervisor was a former Nazi. After World War I, he had emigrated to America, and in 1938 he returned because of his enthusiasm for Hitler. He let me know that I was Jewish. When you start a new position, you need help – he, however, caused problems for me whenever he could.

I liked the city. We shared a house with another family, but we often quarreled over the use of the yard and other trivial things. After the war there was much more quarreling going on in Austria and Germany. The general edginess was probably a consequence of the war and defeat. In any case, I didn't want to stay in Munich or in Germany. I remembered the Austrian vice-chancellor Pittermann again and wrote him another letter, in which I told him what had been happening in the meantime.

Vienna, 1962

Pittermann invited me to Vienna and made an appointment with me. He replied in such a familiar manner that I took heart and purchased a train ticket. He met with me for ten minutes and since he was Minister of State-Owned Concerns, he proposed to get me a job with the railway or the postal service.

Finally we agreed on the idea that I should get transferred to the Vienna branch of Brown-Boveri. When the conversation turned to finding a suitable apartment, coincidence played a big part. The building where my parents had lived and in which I had spent a big part of my childhood and youth had been destroyed by a bomb. A municipally owned apartment building had just been constructed on that exact spot. Pittermann procured an apartment for me on the very same floor where I had once lived with my parents and my sister. That made up my mind for me. I didn't feel that I was being granted a favor, but that I was entitled to it. Today I'm sure that I wouldn't have returned if Pittermann hadn't taken care of everything for me. My dislike of bureaucracy would have gotten in the way, not a hatred of Austria.

The Move

It didn't upset me that the house in which I had lived as a child had disappeared. Rather, I regarded it as a punishment for the tenants who had moved in after us. In any case I was happy that I now lived in an area where I knew my way around. I was sent to the director of Brown-Boveri who hired me as an engineer. The salary was low considering the time, but I eagerly accepted the position, since I was finally able to do work for which I had been trained, and the name of the company was well respected. Four weeks later my wife moved to Vienna with the children and all our belongings.

A Stranger in Vienna

During my visit to Vienna some years earlier I had felt like a stranger the entire time. I knew back then that hardly any Jews lived in Vienna anymore. However, my knowledge had only been theoretical. But now that I had returned for good, this fact became shockingly clear to me. From then on for a long time I disliked the residents of this city. A Viennese doctor I consulted, who was hooked on morphine, prescribed the anti-depressant Preludin for me so I could better deal with my depressions. Initially I took one pill a day, then two, and in the end, three; however, the doctor died after a year, and I had to do without medication from then on. For the most part Preludin gave me more self-confidence and helped me not feel so tired. I liked what I saw in the mirror and was more optimistic about overcoming my problems. At first I had tried to isolate myself. Every time I went outside I had an eerie feeling. I would then think to myself that I shouldn't have come back, realizing that my return had been a mistake.

I didn't feel any hatred; I just found evidence everywhere that what had once been was irrevocably a part of the past. Strangely enough, these experiences made me feel Jewish again. In England I hadn't had any contact with Judaism.

Jewish Life

Every Friday night I went to the synagogue on Seitenstettengasse. I registered with the Jewish community and I went to hear the service. Hearing the Hebrew prayers particularly moved me. Only a few old people participated in the service. Evidently there were no young people anymore and I had the impression that the Jewish community in Vienna was going to die out with my generation (it was only with the arrival later of the refugees from Hungary and Czechoslovakia that the religious community was replenished and life was brought back into it).

After temple I went to City Park. Looking at the passersby, I thought, "They are responsible for it." I felt like a ghost. Of course the move had brought on these thoughts because I had no money and was therefore forced to remain in Vienna. Only my British passport gave me a feeling of security. I asked myself over and over again what it was that had brought me back. I came to the conclusion that it was my roots: the language in particular – but also the city and a certain feeling of familiarity. True, the Jews had disappeared and the non-Jews had become strangers to me — but the parks, the streets, Kahlenberg, the Danube . . . They too are part of a person's homeland, it's not just the people. Moreover, I was curious about future experiences.

At that time, however, a mistrust arose in me that has remained with me until today: a mistrust of national costumes and loden coats or women wearing folkloric hats and feathers . . . It does happen on occasion that when I do speak with such a person in a national costume he smiles at me, to my surprise. By the way, I myself sometimes wear an Austrian folk jacket – "my camouflage coat" – in order not to attract attention.

Searching for Traces

The remaining ruins didn't evoke my sympathy. Quite the contrary, I thought: Not enough! For days I went around Leopoldstadt and was only gradually able to understand the extent of the destruction. Resignedly I noticed that the Jewish orphanage had been turned into a commercial laundry. In front of the house where my grandmother had lived, I was overcome by such profound sadness that I couldn't go in at first. Later I climbed the stairs to the second floor. At that moment a door opened and a woman appeared in the hallway. I asked her how long she had been living here, and she replied since 1939. I turned around. I happened to glance through the hallway window into the former yard. It was now a garage. I felt satisfied that it, too, had disappeared.

Experiences

I wasn't surprised any longer when I saw swastika graffiti; I felt contempt. I mistrusted the country and all Austrians. At the newspaper stands I found the nationalistically-oriented newspaper for veterans freely displayed despite the fact that even then it was notorious for its anti-Semitism. For that reason I bought it almost every week for one or two years, but I hadn't thought it possible that something like it would still find an audience. Later I went in search of Jewish friends from my school days. I didn't find a single one. I met only an old lady, Olga Bader, who had owned Café Augarten. During the war she had escaped to Israel, but since she didn't like it there, she had returned to Vienna in the fifties. (In addition she received her pension in Vienna.) I visited her several times on Negerlegasse. When we talked, I always told her how sorry I was that I hadn't stayed in England.

For five or six years I regretted having returned, and only gradually did I come to terms with my situation.

About Vienna

In comparison with London, I found Vienna provincial. In particular I missed the mix of nationalities. Moreover, people in

England had been more relaxed. They had also been proud of having defeated the Nazis, while everyone in Vienna still complained about what they had to go through with the Russians. When the complaints got too much for me, I interjected: "Most likely the Germans didn't behave much better in Russia." But nobody liked to hear that. Olga Bader, on the other hand, liked to live in Vienna despite the fact she wasn't able to make friends. Everyday she went to her coffeehouse. She was very lonely and lived only in the past. All her relatives had been killed.

One day, with the help of a telephone directory, I traced my cousin Erika. She ran a little antique store. Being half-Jewish, she had remained in Vienna during the war, because she had been baptized as a child and had been in possession of fake documents. That had protected her. Our meeting was a joyous occasion. She hated the Nazis, but didn't want to have anything to do with Orthodox Judaism either. Finally I also tried to contact a non-Jewish schoolmate. I wrote him a letter (from what I had heard he had become a police officer in the meantime). He replied that he didn't remember me and also didn't want to have anything to do with me.

It was only thanks to my wife, who was a Christian in the best sense of the word, that I didn't become anti-Austrian. Anti-Semitism is so deeply rooted within the Austrian population that they don't even realize it. I only need to think of various linguistic expressions. For example, the clitoris is called "Jew" in Vienna . . . A cigarette which is not properly lit is also called "Jew" . . . You can hear the expressions "Jewish haste" or that things are wild "like a Jewish School" . . . When I went to a reunion with former classmates at the Arsenal, I was the only Jew who was left from our class. Our meeting was evidently an embarrassment to my former classmates, nothing else, and I told myself that I had to forget that I knew them. Of course I also looked up our custodian, Mr. Wessely. To my delight he hadn't changed. He had retired from driving a streetcar and now cursed the Social Democrats because they, too, had members who were anti-Semitic. He was surprised that I had returned at all, and I more or less had to apologize for it. He was the only one I met who felt for the Jews and their fate.

Austrian Citizenship

Soon after my return, Pittermann got me Austrian citizenship. I wouldn't have accepted it if I had had to give up my British citizenship. Even today I would rather relinquish my Austrian citizenship than my British citizenship, because if I were forced to leave the country again, I would at least have a British passport.

Out in the Country

Brown-Boveri brought electricity to the most remote villages and farm houses. Every other month we went to a construction site in Carinthia. Compared to the Viennese, the people in the federal provinces seemed more innocent to me. The Viennese always appeared insincere to me, with their supposed recognition of the cultural achievement of Jews on one hand and their covert or open anti-Semitism on the other. I liked going to the country. I never experienced any anti-Semitism, although I know that it existed there, too.

Work

The leader of our group, a Socialist, didn't like Jews in general. When he spoke about someone with influence, he called him a "court Jew," whether he was Jewish or not. But within the group there were never any anti-Jewish remarks. Because of the holy days, I had to report my religion when I started working there — thus everyone knew I was Jewish. In the cafeteria, however, we came across many groups who didn't know me. Once there had been a newspaper article about a memorial ceremony at Mauthausen, site of a concentration camp. In response a worker from another group said, "They couldn't have gassed so many if hundreds participated in the memorial." I didn't put up with his remark, and the man apologized. If anti-Semitic remarks were made, protest came mostly from just one man, a man from Frauenkirchen in Burgenland. He was a helpful and kind man who admitted that the existence of concentration camps was already known during the war. He told me there had been an expression: "Be quiet or you'll leave the house through the chimney!" By the way, before the war, there had been a Jewish community in Frauenkirchen – it had disappeared.

My Family

After my two daughters, my wife gave birth to our son Walter, our daughter Dorli, and lastly, to the twins Mirjam and Regina. As soon as my children were six years old, I sent them to the *Shomer,* which now existed as a Jewish island in a big Aryan sea.

Ten years ago my wife died from cancer. It was a terrible blow. All our children were still dependent on us. My colleagues at work sympathized with my fate; they even collected money for me.

After the funeral, I intended to emigrate to Israel together with the children. I felt that it would be easier to take care of them in the kibbutz. But I still had to work for two years before I could retire. Up to that point since my return to Vienna I hadn't joined any Zionist organization, but after my wife's death I turned with renewed force to religion.

Walter

My son Walter was born in 1962. Like all of my children, he was baptized a Catholic in accordance with my wife's wishes. After her death my children left the Catholic church and became Jewish according to their and my wishes. Walter was fifteen years old at that time. Like me, he went to elementary school on Kleine Sperlgasse.

It all seemed as if nothing had happened. (However, when I had gone to my old elementary school to get my report cards, I was told with faked indignation they couldn't be given to me. The Jews had used them for heating material when they were locked up in the building before their deportation in 1939.)

After elementary school Walter went to high school on Stubenbastei. Like my other children he also went to the *Shomer*.

Even before graduating from high school, he went to Israel on vacation and returned full of enthusiasm. At home he would listen for hours to the music tapes he had brought back from his trip. He told me he wanted to emigrate. I advised him, however, to study first in Vienna. He majored first in history and political science, but soon changed his major to Jewish Studies. I would have preferred to see him study something practical like business or engineering. But Walter wouldn't go along with that.

He was friends with Olga since high school. She came from a Russian-Jewish family and worked later as a translator of Russian and Spanish.

After graduating from high school, Walter stayed in Israel for a year, where he was trained as a youth leader. Among other things he became fluent in Hebrew. Olga visited him twice while he was there. Even back then he was indecisive and suffered from depression, but by the same token, he couldn't be swayed easily from his opinion. After he attended seminary in Israel, he went through a religious phase. He followed strictly the rules of the Sabbath, and during morning prayers he put on the prayer straps, the teffilin. In addition he ate vegetarian food, because he was opposed to the killing of animals. He didn't smoke, hardly drank, and never took any drugs. His political views were both Zionist and Social Democratic.

Basically he came across as cheerful. But at the same time he was also often distracted and didn't answer your questions, so you had to ask him a second time . . . I had to ask him over and over again. (It was as if you had to wake him from a dream.)

Finally, he went to Israel a third time, this time to live in a kibbutz, with the intention of finding out if he wanted to stay or not. Most of the time he was there he drove a tractor. He wrote letters, and Olga visited him. When he returned after a year, he was disappointed with the kibbutz. He told me he couldn't imagine spending the rest of his life like that. Above all he had imagined the kibbutz to be more brotherly. Probably he had idealized it too much.

Walter had been treated coolly by the Marxist group. You get a better reception in a religious kibbutz; they respect you more as an individual.

After his return, Olga and Walter spent everyday together. She was pretty, intelligent, and very ambitious. In the beginning Walter was still undecided about returning to Israel or not. Olga advised against it. He was carrying a plane ticket in his pocket when she hid his passport. After that he went to work for a private security agency.

I was astonished, because as a pacifist he opposed weapons. But he had the goal to earn so much money with the agency that he could pay for his studies . . . Many Jewish students did it this way. He stayed at Olga's frequently and carried his gun with him in a holster. At home he unloaded it and put it in his room. In the summer of 1986 Olga met another man. As a result, Walter moved out, embittered. Nonetheless they parted friends. At that time, Jewish refugees from Iran were waiting in Vienna for permission to emigrate to America. The security agency guarded them because there was the fear of assassination attempts. Walter fell in love with one of the young Iranians and wanted to marry her. A few weeks later she went to America to discuss it with her brothers, who managed a supermarket in Los Angeles. Walter followed her.

He was frostily received. The mentality of the Iranians is different from ours. Moreover, Walter was not wealthy enough for them. Although he had intended to spend more time in Los Angeles, he stayed just a week. When he returned to Vienna he didn't feel at home anywhere anymore. He spent his nights wherever he was at the moment, either at one of his sisters' or at my place. He spent a lot of money calling America, but it was difficult for him to get to speak to the girl. He called Los Angeles on December 22. He only reached one of the two brothers, who stated that his sister wouldn't come to Vienna and that he should leave her alone from then on. Walter was on duty at the Jewish nursing home. At midnight an old man died with whom he had spoken a lot and whom he loved like a grandfather.

The next morning a policeman found Walter dead in the porter's station. He had shot himself through the heart.

Afterwards

At seven o'clock in the morning, my doorbell rang. When I opened the door, I saw Dr. Stein from the Jewish community standing in the stairwell. Two men were waiting behind him. Dr. Stein asked me if he could come in, and I replied it wasn't possible because I wasn't dressed. He then said, "But we have to come in!" I dressed quickly and let Dr. Stein and his companions in. In a very emotional state he informed me what had happened. He said it wouldn't make any sense for me to go to the nursing home, the police had taken the affair in hand. Suicide was suspected from the beginning.

Walter approved of suicide. We had discussed it when Arthur Koestler and his wife committed suicide and again at the time of Jean Améry's suicide. We agreed that your body was your own and what you did to it was nobody else's business.

Dr. Stein and his companions left again. I called my children, one after the other. Lots of errands had to be run. I was paralyzed. In some way it's always the father's fault when a son takes his own life.

The same day his colleagues from the security agency brought two suitcases with his things.

I didn't see Walter again. Among Jews the funeral has to proceed quickly, that's the rule. Many people came to the cemetery, I didn't really take it all in.

After the funeral the rabbi and Walter's friends followed me to my apartment to pray. This was repeated every morning for a week. The apartment was always full of people.

My family has fallen apart now, first because of my wife's death, then because of my son's.

Today I often think that the thing with Walter wouldn't have happened if my wife had been alive.

Every evening for a year I had to recite the Kaddish, which the son usually speaks after his father's death:

"Let the glory of God be extolled, let His great name be hallowed, in the world whose creation He willed. May His kingdom soon prevail, in our own day, our own lives, and the life of all Israel, and let us say: Amen. Let His great name be blessed for ever and ever. Let the name of the Holy One, blessed is He, be glorified, exalted, and honored, though He is beyond all the praises, songs, and adorations that we can utter, and let us say: Amen.

For us and for all Israel, may the blessing of peace and the promise of life come true, and let us say: Amen.

May He who causes peace to reign in the high heavens, let peace descend on us, on all Israel, and all the world, and let us say: Amen."

III

S ome time has gone by since I recorded Berger's story in my notebooks.

I went to the slaughterhouse and to the superior court. They both have more in common than meets the eye. (In one of the many trials that I witnessed, Alois Jenner, a law student from some village, was tried. He was accused of murder.) I have also been to the hostel for the homeless and to the mental asylum (there I met Franz Lindner, another inhabitant of that village who doesn't talk with anyone). I went to Leopoldstadt and climbed St. Stephan's Cathedral. I wrote about it in newspapers and years went by. I have continued to maintain contact with Berger.

Berger told me that Lizzy, the love of his youth, had married a businessman in Chicago and had started a family with him. She and her husband flew to Vienna several times, and together they met Berger at a coffeehouse.

Half a year ago I had an appointment with Berger in front of the Academy of Fine Arts. We wanted to look at Hieronymus Bosch's famous *Last Judgment Triptychon* together. The left part depicts Lucifer's fight with the archangel Michael's host of angels; above it, enthroned in a cloud of light, is God. The fallen and defeated angels are plunging like giant insects into paradise, which spreads out beneath them. In paradise the creation of Eve from Adam's rib is depicted, as well as the fall from grace, and Adam and Eve's expulsion by the archangel Gabriel. Evil was already on earth before Adam and Eve, Bosch says. Evil also existed among God's earlier creatures, namely, the angels who were created before humans. It's almost as if Bosch wanted to show that all of God's creations possessed the potential for evil, and since evil existed as possibility, it became reality. We sat down on the bench in front of the triptychon and read the catalogue that describes and interprets all the details in the paintings. A tumult of creatures can be seen – some more human than animal, some more animal than human, monsters and demons united through violence. Earth is a giant torture chamber in which the tortured are being shod, stabbed, roasted, burned, put through the mincer, broken on the wheel, pierced by arrows, and drowned in feces. The massacre continues in hell, only there God doesn't preside over it, but Lucifer, the fallen carrier of light, who has started his reign.

"Earth is hell," Berger said in the quietness of the picture gallery, in which only the wooden floor squeaked, when the guard shifted his weight from one leg to the other.

A couple days later Berger called me and told me that Lizzy had come to see him. He went on to say that her husband had died a year ago and that she had to take care of his estate with his German relatives. Thus she had taken advantage of the opportunity for a side trip to Vienna. Today she has returned to America, but she promised to come back.

I didn't feel like waiting for the end of his story with Lizzy. Instead, I started to write about Berger's life at the very moment when he had hit the ground after an infinitely long plunge and had miraculously risen again.

Afterword

Gerhard Roth ranks among the most significant contemporary writers of Austrian literature. Like many writers of his generation, his literary beginnings were shaped by a group of avant-garde writers and artists who called themselves the "Grazer Gruppe." In 1959 Alfred Kolleritsch, a writer and native of Graz, founded "Forum Stadtpark" (City Park Forum) as an informal meeting place for the artists who formed this group. At the same time, he published their work in his literary journal *manuskripte* and thus made them known to a larger audience.

The strong interest in the aesthic questions of literary production which characterized the "Grazer Gruppe" has remained important to Gerhard Roth. His style has evolved from a highly experimental beginning to a more conventional narrative form. In some of his later works Roth combines experimental and traditional narrative strategies. He claims that he strives above all to find the styles most suitable for his particular topics. Although varied in style, Roth's work is characterized by its thematic continuity. In all his works the author rejects conformity and a narrow definition of reality. His protagonists strive for definition of self in a world whose cold, impersonal rationality and normative tendencies make for an alienating, hostile, and often destructive environment. In his early works Roth focuses on the subjective inner worlds of his protagonists and their attempts to counteract the hostile forces of society. In his later works, which comprise the cycle *Die Archive des Schweigens* (The Archives of Silence), his interest shifts to the social and political structures of his native Austria.

The five novels in the seven work cycle are *Der Stille Ozean* (The Calm Ocean, 1980), *Landläufiger Tod* (Common Death, 1984), *Am Abgrund* (At the Abyss, 1986), *Der Untersuchungs-richter. Die Geschichte eines Entwurfs* (The Investigating Judge. The History of a Sketch, 1988), and *Die Geschichte der Dunkelheit*

(The Story of Darkness, 1991). The novels are framed by the photo-essay volume *Im tiefen Österreich* (In the Depths of Austria, 1990) and the essay collection *Eine Reise ins Innere von Wien* (A Journey inside Vienna, 1991). *In the Archives of Silence* Roth investigates in particular the role of National Socialism in Austrian history and its consequences in the present.

The destructive forces of National Socialism constitute the central theme of *The Story of Darkness,* but rather than critizing the fascist state directly, Roth focuses on the faith of one of National Socialism's victims, a Viennese Jew. Roth got the idea for this work during a walk in Vienna, when he came across an abandoned Jewish cemetery, which to him symbolized both Austria's historic guilt as well as its failure to take responsibility for it honestly. He wanted to tell the story of a victim of this past, a Viennese Jew who because of his religion and race had to flee the country to save his life and who finds little changed upon returning from his forced exile. Roth's editor introduced him to the man who became Karl Berger. It is true that in comparison with the fate of other victims of National Socialism Berger's does not seem very extraordinary. He is one of the lucky ones: he did not have to suffer the horrors of a concentration camp, and indeed the majority of his family was able to survive the Nazi terror. Yet Roth's work proves the error of such a notion, for even without the experience of the concentration camp, Berger has been branded for life. The forced emigration has not just interrupted his life for a little while but has destroyed it irretrievably. It meant the loss of "Heimat," or a sense of belonging which resulted in a permanent crisis of identity.

Roth presents the story as a series of installments ("reports") narrated by the protagonist. The first two installments establish Berger's identity before his forced exile. It is clearly an Austrian as well as a Jewish identity. His ancestors originated from the eastern part of the monarchy and had successfully settled in the capital of the Austrian empire. They were loyal monarchists as is evident in the account of his grandfather who faced financial ruin after he had bought war bonds in support of the Habsburg monarchy. Berger's childhood does not differ from that of other Austrian children. He has Jewish and non-Jewish playmates and plays the traditional games every Austrian child knows. However, these innocent children's games serve as premonition of the future fate of the Jews. The game of "Is the black cook in?" ends with one child remaining in the center while the others dance around it yelling "There she is, there she is! Yuck, yuck, yuck!" The game of "Hopscotch," too, can be read as a symbol of the future. In life Berger is unable to accomplish the objective of the game: to avoid hell.

While the first report establishes Berger's Austrian identity, the second provides the reader with insight into his Jewish one. Here we find a description of Jewish holidays and traditions as well as an explanation of their origin and meaning. Roth makes a point of emphasizing the close relation between Jewish religion and history: "The history of the Jewish religion is simultaneously the history of the Jews." The author attempts clearly to explain the "otherness" of the Jews through their past history. In this report, documenting differences between Jewish Austrians and non-Jewish Austrians, we also encounter the first signs of hostilities towards Jews. The SA invades Leopoldstadt and Berger starts to sense the anti-Semitism of his teachers and fellow students. He loses hope of being accepted as an Austrian and turns to his Jewish identity: "It became clear to me that I was a Jew and I began to accept it."

His subsequent experiences, however, prevent a positive identification with his Jewish identity. He sees the humiliation of the Jews at the hands of the Viennese on the night of the Anschluss. This marks the beginning of the odyssey, which takes him all over Europe and as far as Canada and Israel. It ends in 1960 with his return to Vienna. Between his flight and his return lie separation from his family and his fiancee, life as refugee, a marriage out of loneliness, fighting against Nazi Germany as a member of the Czech exile army, reunification with his mother and sister, divorce, an unsuccessful attempt to find a new life in Israel, and, finally a promising new marriage.

At each stage of his exile Berger loses part of his identity, and at each stage he realizes anew that he is an outsider. He is tolerated, but not welcomed. He attempts to find a positive identity within his religion and the new countries, but fails. Even in the Czech exile army he is met with anti-Semitic sentiments that prevent a feeling of belonging. His reactions show the discouraging effect of these experiences and the resulting loss of identity: "At that time I would have preferred not to be Jewish. I didn't intend to abandon Judaism, but the anti-Semitism hurt me. I didn't know who I was anymore. Was I an Austrian? A Czech? Was I a Jew? Or was I already British? I had to be something, I told myself."

Berger's many love affairs are a reflection of his identity crisis. None of them can fulfill his longing for love and security, because he withholds himself. It seems that he has finally found peace in his second marriage, but his frequent change of jobs indicates his persistent restlessness.

The Austrian writer Jean Améry, who also had to flee the Nazis, describes Berger's experience of not belonging as characteristic of those who had to leave their native countries in 1938. In his essay *Wieviel Heimat braucht der Mensch?* (How Much *Heimat* Does a Person Need?), Améry defines "Heimat" not as a geographical place, but as a feeling of well-being and security resulting from the knowledge of being a legitimate and accepted member of a community.[1] This security is based on a person's ability to "decode" his or her environment. Améry maintains that the emigrants were able to obtain the semiotic competence to survive in their new environment, but this remained an intellectual and never a spontaneous process and thus prevented the emotional feeling of security. Accordingly, the emigrants not only lost their homes but also their memories because what happened afterwards proved that those memories were based on false conceptions.

---

1. Jean Améry. "Wieviel Heimat braucht der Mensch?" *Jenseits von Schuld und Sühne.* München: Szczesny, 1966, p. 79.

Berger's experiences exemplify Améry's observations. Returning to Austria does not afford him the peace he had hoped for. He cannot suppress his distrust of those who were responsible for the fate of the Jews. At the same time, the Austrians show their distrust, ignorance, and hostility. It is commonly believed that the emigrants had a good life abroad, while those who remained had to live with the dangers and suffering of war. Everyone focuses on private miseries; no one is willing to accept responsibility for what happened during the Nazi reign. It also becomes clear to Berger that anti-Semitism has outlasted the war. The walls are again covered with swastikas, and newsstands are selling anti-Semitic newspapers. He again feels like an outsider.

Berger's attempt to regain part of his identity by returning to Austria fails not just because of the hostility of the Austrians. The new state does little to encourage its former Jewish citizens to return. On the contrary, it is busily erasing any signs of a Jewish presence in the country. During his unsuccessful search for the past, Berger discovers that not only the Jewish people but Jewish culture as well has disappeared from Vienna: Where his school had once stood there is now a construction site, the synagogue which was burned down during *Kristallnacht* has not been rebuilt. He has to accept that the way of life he had known as a youth is lost forever.

For Jean Améry exile meant a loss of security, belonging, and past, a loss from which he never recovered. It resulted in disorientation, self-denial, and finally self-destruction. He committed suicide in 1978. Roth's protagonist, who was spared the experience of the concentration camp, also shows symptoms of a psychological disorder. He is severely depressed and for a year he takes large doses of anti-depressants. Moreover, his loss of identity and sense of belonging affects the next generation.

Berger's son, born in Vienna in 1962, long after the war, is likewise unable to find a "home" in Jean Améry's sense of the word. Like his father he suffers from restlessness, which leads him to Israel and the United States. Disappointed in love as well, he commits suicide when he is only twenty-five years old. This tragic

114

death emphasizes clearly that the past is not over but still claims its victims in the present. But it is also the reason for Berger's desire that the Jewish people remember the past, because "everyone else will forget anyway, that's the way time goes." With *The Story of Darkness* Roth attempts to make sure that this past is remembered and that the voices of its victims are heard.

Roth's intent to tell Berger's story as "truthfully" or maybe as honestly as possible had consequences for the aesthetic form of the work. The first-person narrator at the beginning of novel declares that he will relate Berger's life story verbatim, because of his belief "that Berger's reports are so exemplary that they transcend the borders between document and literature." Because of the fictitious nature of the introductory part of the novel, this declaration should be taken with a grain of salt. In fact Roth based the narrative form of his novel on a very calculated aesthetic concept. In a monologue about the genesis of *The Archives of Silence*, he relates the problems he experienced when trying to write *The Story of Darkness*.[2] His preoccupation with the story and his lack of distance prevented him from finding an appropriate language for it. An encounter with the work of the sculptor Giacometti, who reduces the human body to tall, thin figures gave him the idea to cut his material radically. Looking at black and white photographs strengthened Roth in his resolve to limit the story to its essential message. Since the story was not simply a portrait of Berger but his entire life story, Roth finally settled on the notion of creating a literary photo-album: "I wanted to structure the story as single pictures, pictures in black and white – as if taken with an amateur camera, blurry but authentic because of it. Not as classical 'beautiful photography' but like a photo from a family album produced by an unskilled hand. I wanted each section of this

---

2. "Reise durch das Bewußtsein. Ein Monolog von Gerhard Roth über *Die Archive des Schweigens,* aufgezeichnet von Kristina Pfoser-Schewig," in Uwe Wittstock (Ed.), *Gerhard Roth. Materialen zu 'Die Archive des Schweigens'*. Frankfurt a. M.: Fischer, 1992, pp. 82-94.

narration to constitute such a picture."[3]

Roth presents Berger's life as a sequence of short scenes. Each scene focuses on one significant experience or event. The simple, understated language contrasts with the extraordinary content. But Roth chooses not to exploit the emotional potential of the story. It is up to the reader to supply the unexpressed pain and to understand and dignify the immense suffering contained in each of the literary snapshots. The result is a narrative that transcends a truthful protocol of a real life story. With his portrayal of Karl Berger's life, Gerhard Roth has succeeded in presenting a case study of a Jewish fate as the result of past and present failures of humanity.

Helga Schreckenberger
Univesity of Vermont

---

3. Ibid., p.93 (my translation).